The Force Within

*From police officer
to Paralympian*

Carol Cooke AM

Published by Brolga Publishing Pty Ltd
ABN 46 063 962 443
PO Box 452
Torquay Victoria 3228
Australia

email: markzocchi@brolgapublishing.com.au

All rights reserved. No part of this publication may be reproduced, stored in a retrieval system or transmitted in any form or by any means electronic, mechanical, photocopying, recording or otherwise without prior permission from the publisher.

Copyright © 2021 Carol Cooke

National Library of Australia
Cataloguing-in-Publication data
    Carol Cooke, author.
    ISBN 9781920785031 (paperback)

 A catalogue record for this book is available from the National Library of Australia

Printed in Australia
Cover Photo Credits:
    In police uniform image: Cynthia Banks
    Cycling image: Arnaud Domange
    Medal image: Paralympics Australia
Cover design by WorkingType Studio
Typesetting by Scott Riddle

BE PUBLISHED
Publish through a successful publisher
National Distribution to Australia & New Zealand
International Distribution to the United Kingdom
Ebooks Worldwide
Sales Representation to South East Asia
Email: markzocchi@brolgapublishing.com.au

DEDICATION

I would like to dedicate this book to my grandparents, Hughie, Edna, Anna, Fred and Elizabeth, all of whom were trailblazers in their own right.

To my parents, Donald and Phyllis, thank you for providing me with an amazing family life, growing up, and for instilling in me the ability to be the best that I could be.

To my sister, Cynthia, who has been my best friend and confidant over the years, thank you for being there even when I was your big sister and not so nice to you!

And to my brother, Brian, who I didn't know until I was about 12 but who taught me that there is no such thing a disability, thank you.

Without all of you in my life, I would not be the person that I am today.

Table of Contents

INTRODUCTION 1

PART 1 – THE EARLY YEARS
1. Stepping Into The Unknown 7
2. Knowledge vs Skill vs Wisdom 15
3. Courage To Change Your Life 25
4. Lessons From My Father 35

PART 2 – FAMILY AND CAREER
5. Family Life Lessons 51
6. Sisters Are Forever 55
7. Doing Things Differently 63
8. My Own Learning Begins 69
9. Life In Uniform 79
10. Life On The Street 85
11. Prostitution And Pimps 91
12. Drug Squad Life 105
13. Criminal investigations 117
14. Travel Adventures 125
15. Unexpected Love 137
16. The End Of An Era 145

PART 3 – A NEW LIFE BEGINS
17. Unexpected Changes 151
18. One Life — Live It 159
19. Chasing Dreams 167
20. Life As A Rower 173
21. Cycling Journey 183
22. Chasing The Ultimate Dream 189
23. The Road To Rio 197
24. Adversity Into Advantage 203

CONCLUSION 209
ACKNOWLEDGEMENTS 213
CAROL'S ACCOMPLISHMENTS 215

INTRODUCTION

This book is about how I transitioned from what I thought would be a life-long career as a police officer to living the life as an elite Paralympic athlete. It is about the lessons I have learned from my family's 85 years of service on the Toronto Police Force, and my own. It is about building resilience.

I have learned that when one door closes, another one can open. You may have to look for that door and pull it open, but when you are faced with a change or adversity in life, there can be good things waiting for you on the other side. Step through that door, maybe into the unknown, but embrace what can happen on your life road.

My time on the police force and the lessons that I learned from a family dedicated to this job definitely shaped the person I am today as an athlete, a daughter, a sibling, a friend and a wife. They taught me to be resilient and to look for the good in everything, live with change and accept challenges with open arms. They also taught me about love, unconditional love for family and friends — the type of love that will carry you through the good and the bad times.

I would never go back and change any of my experiences. They have taught me a lot about dedication, integrity, perseverance and belief in myself to see what life had in store for me.

The year 2020 was supposed to be exciting and fulfilling: a swansong to the last ten years of hard training and commitment. The Tokyo Paralympics would be my third games, and at the age of 59, I was still shaking my head in amazement as to what I had accomplished over those last ten years. Not that I didn't think it would happen; I knew my abilities. But at a time when friends my age were looking at retirement, I was still enjoying training and racing against competitors who were, on the whole, a lot younger than me.

At the beginning of January, news out of China was reporting on a new virus that was spreading. To be honest, I don't think I took much notice. The world had been through a number of things like this in the past, such as SARS and Ebola, and I, along with many others, just figured it was another form of flu and that it too would pass.

On 17 March, as the virus became a pandemic and spread from China to Europe, becoming devastating in Italy, I was involved in a teleconference with athletes from around the world and the International Paralympic Committee (IPC) on just what was happening with the games. The word was that there was no plan B and the games would be held. Even though Italy was really in trouble, I thought that I could still head to Europe for the racing season. I would just do some races in other parts of Europe and then head to Belgium to meet the rest of the Australian Para-cycling team for the World Championships.

But on that call, there was an athlete from Italy who pleaded with the IPC. They asked how the games could take place in a way that would be fair to everyone, with some countries not having access to training at all. It was then I knew in my heart that the games wouldn't be going ahead. Weeks later, the IPC informed the world that the games would be postponed to 2021.

At least, we had an answer. Postponed was better than cancelled. My swansong dream was not lost. It was heartbreaking though. As the pandemic spread, the world became more contagious, with thousands dying. At that point, I knew my whole year had been upended. I do believe that life is more important than sport, but when you focus all your energy into a goal and you have timelines in place for an entire year, how do you realign that year?

For someone of my age and background, I was luckier than most. I finished my education. I've had careers and I hadn't put my future on hold. I was doing what I loved, but the younger

Introduction

athletes who had nothing but Tokyo on their minds were lost — athletes who had put university, careers and life on hold to focus on that one goal.

Para-athletes are resilient though; they have been through tough times in life and have made it through the other side. We are a global family that sticks together and helps each other through the good and the bad times, so I knew we would get through this.

We have all faced the unknown in 2020. For me, the uncertainty lied in the Paralympic games and whether they would actually go ahead in 2021. If not, would their postponement take me on an entirely new journey? Of course, there was also the unknown of what the world would be like after this pandemic receded. What would the new normal look like?

Only time will tell, but at least I have the lessons and wisdom learned from years gone by. They have been passed down through the generations from family members who are now a distant memory. Stepping into the unknown was what I was now facing.

I hope that this book will help you face the unknown and take a leap of faith into the future.

> *'Sometimes good things fall apart so better things can fall together.'*
> ~ MARILYN MONROE

PART 1
The Early Years

CHAPTER 1

Stepping Into The Unknown

'A journey of a thousand miles begins with a single step.'
~ LAO TZU

My grandfather, Hugh James Mackey Banks, was born in Caithness, Scotland, on 15 January 1907, to parents, Isabella and Hugh Banks. He was one of nine children. In 1921, he emigrated to Canada as a teenager, along with his parents, with high hopes of a new life in a faraway land. After arriving and seeing what this new world had to offer, he decided, even at that young age, that when he could, he would join the Third Brigade Field Artillery (Militia). He had always had a love of horses from an early age, and upon arriving in Canada, he took it upon himself to take riding lessons in the University Armouries. He loved these lessons, and his skill and grace on a horse made him a natural rider. Once he felt he was proficient on the back of a horse, he, in fact, did join the Militia.

The Early Years

With more training upon joining the Militia and upon graduating as a skilful horseman, he was sent to the R.C.H.A. riding establishment at Kingston, Ontario, where he graduated as a rough-riding corporal. He joined one of Canada's crack cavalry regiments, the Royal Canadian Dragoons (Permanent Force), serving there until 1929 when he joined the Toronto City Police as Police Constable #631, where he served 33 years.

Grandad's love of horses saw him join the Mounted Unit, and he loved patrolling the city of Toronto on horseback. During his time policing, he came to know the local community where he was working, and they came to know him as the young good-looking officer from Scotland.

On 31 December 1929, the local community was having a New Year's Eve celebration at the Canadian Legion Hall. Hughie, as he was affectionately known, dressed in his finest brown pin-striped suit, a crisp, freshly starched white shirt, with his tie neatly tucked in his vest and his hat on his head, was heading to the celebrations. He put his warm overcoat on and braved the cold winds of the winter night as he walked toward the hall. He had no idea that this night was going to be a changing point in his life.

As he entered the hall, celebrations were well under way, and he headed to the coat check to drop off his hat and overcoat. Waiting in line, he noticed that the coat check was being manned by a beautiful young woman, strikingly tall, with dark brown hair and the face of an angel. With his coat and hat in his hand as he approached the counter, he found himself lost for words, which was something new to him. As he handed his items to this beautiful young woman, his voice returned, and he asked her what her name was.

'Edna,' she replied with a smile that could light up a room.

'Nice to meet you. I'm Hughie,' he said.

There was no time for further conversation as the people behind him wanted to drop off their items and get into the celebrations. He was tongue-tied anyhow and wasn't sure what to say next.

As he entered the hall with the festivities, music and dancing in progress, all he could think of was Edna. After a couple of hours and a few glasses of beer, Hughie had gained a bit of courage, so he headed back out to the coat check where Edna was now sitting with another woman, chatting. Hughie approached her, took a deep breath and asked her if she could come and have a dance with him. Edna, with that beautiful smile, turned to her co-worker and with a nod of her head turned to him and said yes.

As Edna made her way out of the little coat check booth, Hughie could feel his legs trembling. He silently scolded himself for his nerves; after all, he was a big burly policeman! But Edna was beautiful. He felt like he had fallen in love without even knowing her, and this was a new feeling for him. They got to the dance floor, and the band began to play the song 'When You're Smiling' by Louis Armstrong. Hughie took Edna in his arms and began to dance. The hall was crowded and noisy, but it felt as though they were alone in the room. He just could not stop looking at this beautiful woman's smile. He knew that they were destined to be with each other.

They had a few more dances before the countdown to midnight began. As the jubilant celebrations gathered speed and noise, the clock hit twelve and Hughie took Edna in his arms and kissed that beautiful face. Edna reciprocated by wrapping her arms around his neck, for she too felt what Hughie was feeling. This was a union that was meant to be, and from that night onwards, they became inseparable.

Every bit of time Hughie had off from work, they would spend together. Edna was only 17 at the time they met, and Hughie turned 23 shortly after their meeting on New Year's Eve. They were caught up in the romance of the relationship. Before too long, Edna had fallen pregnant, at only 17. In the early part of the 1900s, sex out of wedlock was just not heard of very often, but they both knew that there was no one else for either of them

The Early Years

and wanted to marry. Edna's parents were not too happy about the fact that Edna was pregnant. It was scandalous, and they expected Hughie to do the right thing. Her parents wanted them to marry as soon as possible so that the pregnancy wouldn't be showing too much, and both Edna and Hughie assured them that this was their wish as well.

It was a rush to get them married, after having known each other for only three months. On 24 March 1930, Hughie and Edna, then one month pregnant, were married, and it was almost eight months to the day after their marriage that their first child, Barbara, was born. They went on to have two more children, both boys: Edward (Eddie, as we all knew him) born in 1933 and my dad, Donald (Don), born on 31 January 1934.

Grandpa's love of horses was so strong that he ended up moving his young family to the Sunnybrook Farms to train the police horses. He had such a great background with horses during his military career that he was asked to take over the training of the 50 police horses that were housed here. They had a small house on the property, and from all accounts, life was pretty good.

Life took a cruel turn when in 1939 war broke out and Hughie went overseas. While he was away, Edna died suddenly, at the age of 27, on 23 October 1940. Edna's death was listed as epilepticus. She had a seizure and fell down the stairs, hitting her head on the way down. It is unsure whether Edna and her family knew she had epilepsy or not. It is possible that they did and had kept it a secret. In the 1930s, epilepsy was still thought to have links with socioeconomic background, and patients were regarded as 'not too bright'. Edna would have been taught from a young age not to let anyone know about her condition.

With their father overseas fighting a war, the three children were split up amongst relatives until he was able to return. As a six-year-old, Dad went to live with his Aunt May and Uncle Bob Gray, Edna's oldest brother, in York, without his brother and sister. His Uncle Bob was employed as a fireman and lived right across the street from the firehall. One of Dad's first memories was how his Uncle Bob would take him down to the Runnymede Presbyterian Church to Sunday school. This was the start of his regular associations with churches throughout his life.

This wasn't a great time for the family, even though Dad had a roof over his head and food to eat with his aunt and uncle. While his father was away, his grandfather sold all their possessions, including the family home.

Within a year of his wife's death, Hughie returned home from the war due to an accident during which his left leg was crushed by a gun-carrier wheel. He needed to recover from his injuries. But upon his arrival home, he found that the love of his life, his beautiful Edna, had died. He was devastated and fell into a deep depression. How was he going to get through life without the love of his life? To make matters worse, the injuries that he had suffered during the war meant that he could no longer be an officer on horseback. He found himself without his wife, injuries to his leg, and with three young children to care for. Because his father had sold all their possessions after the death of Edna, he didn't even have a home to raise his young family. Luckily, he was still employed by the Toronto Police Force and was being paid even though he had numerous issues with his damaged leg.

The children were returned to the care of their father, and even though my dad really didn't know his father, he, along with Barbara and Eddie, joined him to live with their grandparents, Hugh Snr and Isabelle Banks. For about two years, they all lived together in a large house in the Woodbine Avenue and Gerrard Street area of Toronto along with their Aunt Chrissie, who was unmarried at the time. This gave Hughie time to recover from his injuries and find a suitable job within the police force. He was determined to get his life back together for the sake of his children.

The Early Years

In 1943, when Dad's aunt Chrissie was about to get married, Hughie felt capable of taking charge of his own life and moved the family into their own home, slightly east at Main and Gerrard Streets. Barbara, who was 13 at the time, took over the household duties for the family but found it very hard to handle this work while also trying to go to school.

Hughie decided that he needed to find a housekeeper who could also act as a babysitter for the children. It was too much to rely on Barbara to do it all and keep going to school. He asked a friend from the police force if he knew of anyone, and he suggested an Irish woman by the name of Anna Forbes who was working as a housekeeper in another part of the city. Anna was contacted, and after meeting Hughie, she agreed to take the job and began immediately. I really think that she took one look at this large good-looking policeman and thought he was a great catch! Needless to say, love soon blossomed between the two of them, and they were married on 30 September 1943.

My dad absolutely loved Anna because she was a fabulous cook and a great homemaker, but her other side, he was not so fond of. She was a very strict disciplinarian and ran the home like a boot camp. But I honestly believe that Anna gave Dad life lessons that he otherwise never would have had.

By 1951, the injuries Hughie had sustained during the war were causing difficulties with his left leg, and it was decided that it would have to be amputated. He was fitted with a very heavy wooden prosthetic leg, but this didn't stop him from continuing to work at the local police station. He refused to be labelled disabled. It was just an inconvenience, and he was bound and determined not to let it stand in his way.

The love of thoroughbred horses was in his blood, and he wanted to continue working with them. A few years went by, and he bought a broodmare and got a foal. He had a good feeling about this foal.

It wasn't until 1962, when he retired from the Toronto Police Force after 33 years of service, that he was able to fulfil a lifelong dream. That foal had grown up to become Admiral's March, a beautiful chestnut brown thoroughbred who that year had two wins, two seconds, two thirds and three fourths.

Racing became not only his passion but Anna's also. All the children had grown up and were leading their own lives, and Hughie and Anna wanted a new adventure together. They worked hard and eventually had a few good race horses and they both got jobs at the Woodbine Racetrack, Hughie doing security work and Anna working in the kitchen area (which she didn't retire from until the age of 86).

Hughie hid his wooden leg so well that many people at the track didn't realise that he was missing a leg until, one day, he took a tumble down a few stairs and ended up with his uniform covered in red clay. His leg had taken a beating, with the left foot facing the wrong way and what looked like his leg snapped just below the knee. People were running around frantically, looking for assistance for 'elderly Hughie, who has broken his leg'.

A wheelchair was found for him, and track workers gingerly picked him up to put him in the chair, trying to be gentle. Most had never seen such a bad break of a leg and couldn't believe that this elderly security guard was so tough and not showing the pain he must have been in. Once in the chair, Hughie reached down and grabbed his leg in both hands just below the point of the break and yanked it sharply back into place. One of the top executives looked at him and asked him if he was okay. Hughie's only reply was, 'I won't be at work tomorrow; I don't have another leg.' That's when they noticed that Hughie indeed had a wooden leg.

So what legacy and lessons did Grandpa Hughie leave me?

Hughie was certainly a character, and I remember sitting on his knees and knocking on the wood of his prosthetic leg. As I sat there

The Early Years

listening to his stories, I learned that, even through adversity, you can accomplish what you set out to do. He taught me to follow my dream, no matter what.

We don't have forever, and life can be unpredictable, so be prepared for the twists in life but don't give up your dreams. Take a chance on that first step, that unknown, but always follow your heart and do something you love.

He also taught me that you can never give up on love. After losing the first love of his life, Edna, he once again fell in love, with Anna. Together, they had 30 wonderful years of following their dreams.

CHAPTER 2
Knowledge vs Skill vs Wisdom

'Do what you can, with what you have, where you are.'
~ THEODORE ROOSEVELT

My dad loved having Anna as his new mother. He loved the fact that she was an incredible cook but wasn't too keen on the fact that she ran the house like a boot camp, with tough rules that were strictly enforced.

Dad had to walk several miles to and from school each day, but he was also, at the age of nine, expected to work and contribute. Never one to complain, he found numerous odd jobs with local businesses, and by the time he was 12, he had jobs before, during and after school. He delivered the paper to

The Early Years

more than 40 customers before school and helped out with the kindergarten children during the school day. Then, after school, he delivered the orders for Gaudin's grocery store until they closed at 6 pm. In the evening, he would deliver orders for Barber's Drug Store until 9 pm.

He also had jobs on the weekends. On Friday and Saturday evenings, he worked as an usher at the Ideal Theatre. When the Strait's Drug Store needed extra help, he would go over and work at the Soda Bar, making sundaes, sodas and banana splits. He also worked for the Magnero family, who ran a grocery store, when they needed an extra hand. On Saturday mornings, he would get there first thing to deliver groceries, but before he was allowed to deliver the orders, Mrs Magnero would ask him if he had had his breakfast. Unfortunately, sometimes he had to truthfully say no, so she would sit him down at her kitchen table and feed him a full breakfast.

Every second week, a wholesale clothing store would require help to stack stock for shipment to retailers, and finally, on a Thursday, Dad and his brother, Eddie, would head over to the local fish and chip store where they would peel 24 huge buckets of potatoes, although I believe they got to eat their fair share of fish and chips!

Talk about a busy young man, who also attended school every day and joined a Boy Scout troupe. But with all these jobs, not only did he help add to the family coffers, but he made enough money to buy all his own clothes. His pride and joy purchase was a specialty first aid kit that he used during his Boy Scout days.

I am convinced that the kindness shown to him by the people who employed him, fed him and believed in him, led him to become one of the most caring and passionate men I have ever had the privilege to know. Witnessing his father's love for his family led him, in turn, to be a great family man.

Knowledge vs Skill vs Wisdom

Later in my life, I realised why my dad was so good with his money: he learned from a very young age that in order to own something you had to work hard for it. He was a pretty resilient kid who carried that through into his adult life, and it is a trait I believe he passed down to my sister and me. During my sister's eulogy to Dad, she said, 'His resilience grew from love and laughter where did that love and laugher come from? It was a gift given to him in return for helping others, and he discovered that secret early around his boyhood neighbourhood. He had the duty, discipline and a responsibility to take action in service work in everyday "normal" life. The stuff you don't get rewards or accolades for. And through it, he found joy.'

After graduating from Kimberly Public School, my dad continued his high school education at Earl Beatty Commercial High School, which was located in the Coxwell and Danforth Avenue's area. He enrolled in the Typing – Stenographic course, a choice which was highly unusual for a boy. But as he told me, he enjoyed it because there were 35 girls in the class and only three boys! When he graduated a few years later, he was an expert at typing, shorthand and filing. His father then organised a job for him with McKim Advertising, which was one of the larger agencies in Toronto, and he was busily engaged in many types of office work for their many clients.

Shortly after starting work at McKim, his father, Hughie, had to have his leg amputated, and while he was in hospital, Dad saw an advertisement in the daily paper: the Toronto Police Department were looking for applicants for police cadets. He went to the police headquarters, filled out an application and soon learned that he had been accepted. How to tell his father was the question.

So, he went to see him in hospital and made up a story of how McKim had fired him. His father asked him why, but without replying to him, Dad told him it was okay, he had another job. When Hughie asked him what it was, Dad told him he had enlisted

The Early Years

as a cadet with the Toronto Police Department, just as he had done many years before. His father said, 'Surely, you can do better than that!' But Dad replied that he himself had been happy with his association with the department, and Dad thought it was a good opportunity to make a career of it. Therefore, on 30 January 1951, on the eve of his 17th birthday, Dad officially joined the City of Toronto Police Department as a 'potential police officer clerk'.

Dad's first duties were to be the mail boy. This entailed delivering mail around the office and dealing with the remaining mail addressed to the police department. Most of these envelopes had money and parking tickets enclosed. After recording them, he would hand them to a man who would put them into an audit book and deposit the money at the bank.

He also had a lot of 'gopher' jobs as ordered by his superiors and was paid the tidy sum of $27 per week. After a few months of this routine work, he learned that the police department was going to install teletyping equipment to connect their various offices. This was going to be a separate unit within the department. As he had been trained in high school for this very work, he decided to ask if he could join the new service. He went to see Chief of Detectives Archie McCathie and enquired about the new teletype branch.

'Oh lad, you can't do that,' McCathie replied. 'You're going to be a good policeman.'

But Dad protested, saying that he had four years to go as a clerk and that maybe, by that time, he wouldn't want to be a policeman. He also mentioned his training as a typist in high school. Secretly, he wanted this job because it paid $20 more per week than his present job, almost double what he was currently earning.

'Lad, where do you want to start, at the top or the bottom?' McCathie said.

'Just anywhere in the teletype unit. That's what I want,' Dad replied.

McCathie then gave him the job on the spot, and he spent the next four years in the teletype department. He had no idea that by taking on this role it would hold him in good favour in years to come and give him opportunities that no one else would get.

At 21 years of age, Dad then entered the police college for more formal training over a period of eight weeks to become a police constable. The college was on the top floor of the headquarters building, and when he graduated, they had a tea party there to celebrate their new status. Not quite today's idea of a celebration!

His first assignment was at the Court Street Police Station at Church Street and King Street. The new constables were paraded out to their posts every day to begin their duties. They would have to march in single file as if on parade, with no talking or any shenanigans. They would then be dispersed from the Adelaide Street and Yonge Street area by their sergeant to their various assigned areas.

At the time, there were only two police cars in the area, so most officers were on foot patrol. Police telephone boxes in various locations allowed them to keep in contact. It was a requirement that they had to ring into the station once before their lunch break and once after to report that 'all was well'. The calls were recorded on teletype, and they didn't need to speak to anyone unless they needed to report an emergency or ask for assistance. The street boxes were quite efficient in summoning a policeman. In the daytime, a loud bell would ring periodically, but at night, so as not to disturb the sleeping community, a red light would go on at the box.

In those days, patrolmen were required to 'work a beat' not 'walk a beat' as the sergeant would not only assign the streets to cover but would also require the officers to gather information from the residents of that street – information such as how many of the commercial places had safes or how many fur coats were displayed in a window. The sergeant would often visit the officers on the beat during the night and question them to determine their alertness. Each officer had to be familiar with the businesses on his beat and the merchandise displayed in each window. One of the big crimes at that time in the city were smash-and-grabs, so officers needed to know what was taken from the window.

The young officers were also meant to check the doors of premises, and if they found an unlocked door, they would get a credit mark on their record. However, if you failed to find an open door and the sergeant did, you would have to make a full report as to why you didn't locate it. It was usually many months before any of the new recruits were ever assigned to a scout car.

The one thing that set Dad apart from the others was his typing ability, which he had become expert at while working in the teletype area. So when there was a serious incident that had to be reported in writing to the chief, other officers would ring all the phone boxes to find Dad and have him come to the station to help with the report writing. This gave him a variety of jobs and kept him abreast of many incidents that were not familiar to other constables. Who would have thought that his decision to join those 35 girls in that class, all those years ago, would pay off so much in the future!

For most of his shifts, Dad would patrol by himself, but on Friday and Saturday nights, they would work in pairs because of the bars. He spent a lot of time calling for a 'paddy wagon' to pick up the local drunks who would sleep it off in the cells. It wasn't a problem if the offender had no identification on him because the veteran officers usually knew them by name.

Dad spent a couple of years working on foot patrol and eventually in the car answering calls for a number of different issues but mostly domestic disputes and break and enters. He was then put into plain clothes within the division where he would check pool halls and bars, uncovering anything related to gambling, bookmaking or morality offences, like prostitution or illegal alcohol. He wouldn't shave and would wear tattered, unkempt clothes and sit on the curb in the

Church Street and Wesley Street area. Local regular drinkers would take him to a bootlegger where he would buy alcohol with marked money. They would then get a search warrant, search the premise, seizing all the alcohol and money. He told me that on a Sunday during the early morning hours you could get five or six different bootleggers.

As Dad was working his way through the police department, he did have a personal life as well. As a teenager and young adult, he always attended church, the Glenmount United Church. It was here that he met a young woman named Adele Darley. When Dad turned 21, they decided to marry, and on 17 February 1957, they had a son, Brian Douglas Banks. Unfortunately, Brian was born with Down syndrome and spent several years in hospital in the Orillia area.

It was shortly after the birth of Brian that Dad learned that Adele was having an affair with the superintendent of the Sunday school. This was a big problem for Dad as in those times the police department frowned upon marital problems and divorce. They had a strict code whereby any officer who was 'consorting with a female other than his wife' could be dismissed. Even though Dad was the victim here, he worried that this would cause him to lose his job.

He confided in the police doctor who had been treating him for a back complaint, and unbeknown to him, the doctor told his inspector. The inspector called him in, gave him information about a good lawyer and told him that the department would have his back during the divorce. So, this was the end of his marriage to Adele. Adele ended up marrying the man she had been seeing, and the two of them raised a family together. Dad kept in touch for Brian's sake but didn't tell me about Brian until I was ten years of age. Once we knew about Brian, he eventually became a part of our family as well.

The Early Years

While Dad's personal life was falling apart, he continued to thrive in the police department, continuing to work in plain clothes, moving from the gambling and bootleggers to prostitution. He always said that those were interesting days because they were always matching wits with lawbreakers. They also used to compete with other police divisions by crossing over the invisible boundary into another station's territory to arrest a bootlegger or prostitutes, which would cause the officers to get into trouble with their own inspector about others cleaning up their area. But the other officers would always retaliate by doing the same thing to them. They certainly enjoyed themselves while working!

Growing up and through his involvement with the church, Dad always thought he might like to become a minister, but I think he found his calling when he first applied to be a cadet. He kept a close link with the church, teaching Sunday school and singing in the choir, and this association continued throughout our lives and until the day he died.

One of his other passions was singing, and as he was involved with the church from a young age, he sang in the choir. This continued into his adult life, and in 1966, he decided to bring it into his policing life by helping found the Toronto Police Male Chorus. The first meeting was actually held in the basement of our house. As the choir grew, so did their reputation, and they were requested to sing at several different venues, not always related to events with the police department.

Some of my fondest childhood memories are of attending various concerts by my dad's choir. I went so often that I knew the words to every song, and I was so proud to see my dad up there in his choir uniform. He loved that choir and sang in it until very late into his career.

Dad always believed that it was important to learn and gain knowledge. Not just learn for skill but also learn for wisdom.

Throughout his career, he enrolled in numerous courses, whether he thought it was something he needed right away or knowledge that he could tuck away in the corners of his brain to assist him in the future.

Dad taught me that you need to have knowledge to gain wisdom. Wisdom is learned over time so that you gain skill by the constant practice of that which you are learning.

'Wisdom is not a product of schooling but the lifelong attempt to acquire it.'
~ ALBERT EINSTEIN

CHAPTER 3
Courage To Change Your Life

'You cannot swim for new horizons until you have courage to lose sight of the shore.'
~ WILLIAM FAULKNER

My mother grew up in Smooth Rock Falls, in far Northern Ontario. It's a small town set in beautiful bushland quite a distance from any big city. The town was the hub for the Abitibi Pulp and Paper Mill, where my grandfather, Fred, worked. Grandpa had gone to Smooth Rock Falls after serving his country in World War I, having heard about work available. Smooth Rock Falls was interesting in itself as it was a small town that was half English and half French.

My grandmother Elizabeth (Betty), born in 1898, had exquisite English manners and was a very gentle soul. In 1923, she immigrated to the United States and worked as a nanny in Rhode Island and then headed to Milford, Massachusetts, where she worked for a family as a cook. She was unhappy and missing home so returned to England in 1925.

The Early Years

However, a year later, she was still searching for some excitement in her life and saw an advertisement for staff needed in the local hotel in Smooth Rock Falls, Ontario, Canada. She knew all the proper things to do: how many glasses should be on the table, which fork was used for which part of the meal, and so on. So, she applied and was given the job of head waitress. But before her mother would let her head to Canada, Betty had to agree to take her younger sister Evelyn with her. She wrote to the hotel, and they agreed to take her sister on as well. Evelyn accompanied Betty on her voyage to the wilderness of Canada.

I remember her describing her journey of their ocean crossing with a smile on her face and a gleam in her eye. She described how the journey was rough and Evelyn was quite seasick but that she, herself, had partied the entire way! It was not a journey for the faint-hearted. Once they had made the ocean crossing, they had to take a train to Toronto, another into the northern bush, where the line ended, and finally a horse-drawn wagon into Smooth Rock Falls. It was many weeks before they arrived, but when they did, they were greeted by the hotel owners and put right to work. This is where Fred and Betty met for the first time. Fred, being a bachelor, took all his meals at the hotel, so they met as soon as Betty started working there. They became friends and eventually love blossomed, but they didn't marry until Betty became pregnant and they knew that they had to. They were married on 12 February 1931, when Betty was two months pregnant. So worried was my grandma about being pregnant before her marriage that she even changed the year of their marriage in the family bible so that it looked as though they were married in 1930. This seems to have been a theme in my family, with grandmothers on both sides falling pregnant before marriage.

Their first daughter, Elizabeth, was born at the end of August 1931, and Grandma being 33 years old, they didn't waste any time starting the rest of their family. They went on to have three more children: Rheta, born in 1932; Marjorie, born in 1934 and my mother, Phyllis, who was born on 2 May 1936. Unfortunately, they lost a son at birth between Rheta and Marjorie, but their family of six was complete. As a family in such a small town, they were the envy of the locals because my grandfather believed in always keeping the family together. Instead of spending his time in the beer parlours with his co-workers at the mill, he would teach his children about the world around them. He would take them into the wild bush and teach them about the different trees, the birds and talk about the many earthly things there.

He planted a big garden in the bush where he grew potatoes, carrots and turnips for their winter storage and taught them how to look after the garden. The sisters remember going into the bush to pick wild blueberries for their mother but had to take old brooms in case the bears came out so they could chase them away. Keeping an eye out for bears and trying to load up their baskets with blueberries was fun, or so they thought back then. They never did see a bear but plenty of little foxes.

Fred taught his daughters how to ski and play tennis, and he sat with the girls while they learned maths, read the Books of Knowledge and gave them the love of books, which they all still have to this day.

Grandpa was a scout leader, and Grandma, a Brownie leader, so the girls all took part, learning from them about semaphore, flags and all the bush info so they could get their badges for Brownies or Guides. Their parents also taught them a love of music as they had to sit quietly and listen to the Singing Stars of Tomorrow, a radio show where all the top singers in the country made their mark.

As the youngest two, Marjorie and my mom had to share a bed until they were 14 and 12 respectively, and like any sisters, they often fought. They had an imaginary line down the middle of the bed, and if one of them crossed it, the kicking would start.

The Early Years

Eventually, when Betty and Rheta moved out, they were allowed to move to the attic, had the whole room as their bedroom and each had their own double bed. They still had an imaginary line but to divide the bedroom. When it was time to clean the room and a piece of paper was on the imaginary line, Marjorie would tear a piece off and leave the rest for my mom as it was not on her half of the room. Thank heavens, as they matured, this stopped, and they became very protective of each other.

The girls attended Smooth Rock Falls Public School and then Smooth Rock Falls Continuation School (high school) where my mom was very sporty, playing hockey as the goalie with Marjorie playing defence. Grandpa would often be a chaperone on the bus if they travelled out of town to play. Mom is the first one to tell you that she wasn't very good or fond of being goalie. She often ducked as the puck headed towards her, but she loved basketball, excelled at it and was very popular in the high school.

Even the town gossip, Mrs Wild, envied the family because they were always together and always said that the children seemed so well-behaved. But they weren't always the perfect family, with fights at the kitchen table and arguments between the girls, just like any family. Grandpa was very strict, and often the girls would catch the end of a rope or twig if they were caught doing something that they shouldn't be doing.

Times were tough financially, and Grandma never let the girls cook as she didn't want to waste any food. She did teach them to make pies and meatloaf. She would send them to the Hudson's Bay store to buy hamburger meat, making sure that they asked the butcher to run it through the grinder twice to make it very lean.

Even when Marjorie left home to become a nurse and it was tough going, Grandma and Grandpa always found the money to buy her proper shoes or a nursing uniform. Mom had wanted to follow in her sisters' footsteps and become a nurse, but she quickly changed her mind when she realised that her parents really couldn't afford it. Instead, she decided to become a teacher.

Phyllis left the safe, comfortable family home and headed to the big city of Toronto to take a summer course learning the basics of teaching and doing some practical work. Those days you were not required to have a degree. It was the first time she had been to Toronto, and although she was a bit nervous about the course, she was excited about being in the big city. Besides, she got to stay with her sister Rheta.

After the course, she was able to head back towards home, where she taught her first year in Nipigon, Ontario. The following summer, she went to Thunder Bay, Ontario, for a second teaching course and then back to Nipigon for another year. After this second year, she was able to go to the North Bay Teacher's College for a year where she received her teaching certificate and was offered a job in Scarborough, a suburb of Toronto.

As Rheta was living in Toronto, Mom moved in with her, right in the heart of the city. The job with the Scarborough Board of Education was at the Scarborough Golf Club Road Public School. After a year, she was getting tired of teaching and really wanted some excitement in her life, at which point she happened to see an advertisement in the Toronto Star newspaper for policewomen. She told Rheta that she was going to apply. This was 1957, and at the time, she was only 21 years old. This was certainly not something that women usually did as a profession, but Mom saw this as an exciting new challenge. She had inherited her mother's sense of adventure and her enthusiasm to step into the unknown.

She didn't want to tell her parents until she knew if she would get the job. After all, they were way up in Northern Ontario, and at this point, what they didn't know wouldn't hurt them.

Phyllis had to head down to 149 College Street, which was police headquarters at the time for an interview. The police officer who interviewed her, Darryl Sewell, would later become a close family

The Early Years

friend I came to know as Uncle Darryl. She was asked about her background and whether she had ever been in trouble with the police, and she was given a few tests such as one for colour blindness. When she found out that she had been accepted, she was excited and nervous, both at the same time. She was tall and very thin, and in the back of her mind, she worried that she wouldn't be up for the challenge.

In 1958, she attended a training centre located near Yonge Street north of Sheppard Avenue on Greenfield Avenue. There were only four other women in the class. The training took place over three months and included classroom work, learning the law and self-defence. However, for the women, the self-defence only included different types of hand holds. At this time, policewomen didn't carry guns but were issued with a small baton that they were trained to use. They also carried a purse to hold the baton along with handcuffs. On 6 October 1958, Phyllis was appointed as a 3rd class policewoman. This was where all officers started, and each year with a favourable review, they would be appointed a higher class, eventually becoming 1st class. Mom was the fourteenth women appointed to the Toronto Police Force.

The uniform the policewomen (PWs) wore consisted of a skirt, blouse and heels of about two inches (old mother shoes, as she called them), cap and purse. If they had to chase someone, they would be hard-pressed to run in their shoes.

Once the training was completed, she was detailed to Court Street Station, Women's Division. As the name suggests, this was a separate division for the women. Her boss was a woman, Sergeant Fern Alexander. Sergeant Alexander was the only sergeant that Phyllis reported to, but the policewomen could be commanded and disciplined by any officer above them, male or female.

She remembers being chastised by another sergeant one day when she was off duty. On her way home, but still in uniform, she had decided to stop into a hairdressing salon. As she was leaving, a male sergeant saw her coming out of the shop and said, 'You are not to go into a place like that in uniform. You can't even go into a restaurant to get a cup of coffee.' The male officers at the time would have been considered to be getting to know their local business owners. Although she was the same rank as her male counterparts, Phyllis and the other women on the police force were treated extremely differently.

They were detailed to direct traffic at the Queen Street 'cattle crossing', as it was known, a major pedestrian crossing between the big shops — Eatons, on the north, and Simpsons, on the south — with cars and streetcars going east and west.

There were numerous days while directing traffic that Phyllis would cop an elbow to the head by someone sitting in the streetcar as it went by. One day she was hit in the head so many times that the next streetcar she saw coming she put her arm up and hit each elbow that was hanging out the windows. She enjoyed this posting and found it interesting, in part because she would meet and see so many people every day. She became such a regular sight at that intersection that the city actually made a safety poster using her image.

Aside from directing traffic, the women would also be walking the beat along with their male counterparts. Phyllis never had to use one of the call boxes around the city to call for help or phone something in. At the time, police officers who were walking a beat didn't carry radios like they do today. The call boxes were direct links to the station if you needed to call for assistance or if you were being assigned a detail or incident to attend.

However, even if Mom did hear it ring and there was a male officer around, the man would be the one to answer it. It certainly was a different world of policing back in the late 1950s.

She worked for a short time at the Old #5 Station off Dundas Street and did get to attend some calls while out in a car, mostly with another woman, but they were never asked to attend

The Early Years

calls that were dangerous. She did at times attend calls with a male officer but never those considered serious, such as armed robberies or emergency calls. Most of the calls that she would attend involved children who had run away or may be in need of protection and needed to go into care.

Mom was well ahead of the times and became one of the first women to work with the Morality Bureau, undercover, investigating so-called 'crimes against morality' such as prostitution. Unfortunately, she doesn't remember a lot of the details of what she did working for the Morality Bureau, but she does recall a couple of incidents.

The Morality Bureau was put together in the late 1800s so the police could watch over parks, dancehalls, taverns and theatres with the aim of putting an end to brothels and arrest women who would be considered to be 'women of the night' working as prostitutes. It also targeted public intoxication, illegal alcohol, gambling and cruelty against women and children, which included abortion and infanticide.

The Morality Bureau continued right into the new millennium but now no longer exists, with crimes such as drugs, gambling and prostitution coming under the Organized Crime Enforcement unit.

Mom does however recall once having to dress up to look like a prostitute, make-up and all. As she got ready at her apartment with Rheta watching on, she was nervous but knew that, as an older sister, Rheta was more nervous about this than she was.

It was believed that a nightclub at Dundas and Yonge Streets was being used by prostitutes to pick up clients. For her job that night, she was told to go into the restaurant area, sit at the bar and wait for a possible client to arrive, to see if she was approached and offered money for sex in return. She was told not to worry: there were going to be people watching her. If she was approached and solicited, she was to leave the club with the 'client' but not to get in a car with them. The 'client' would then be arrested by backup officers.

As she was sitting there, a man walked in whom she realised was from her hometown of Smooth Rock Falls. He recognised her, came around and sat down beside her.

'Phyllis Monkman, how are you?' he asked.

Mom was worried; she hadn't been primed for what to do if this happened. She decided that she had to tell him the truth.

'I'm sorry, but I can't talk to you because I am a police officer and I'm undercover,' she whispered to him.

'Oh, okay,' he replied with a shocked look and left abruptly.

This is where her memory fades about that night, but she does remember leaving the nightclub with a man, walking down the street with a car following her. As the 'client' was arrested, she was told to leave the area by the backup officers.

She also did jobs for the Morality Bureau involving illegal 'booze houses'. She posed drunk with another officer to get in to see if the proprietors were selling alcohol illegally. To me, my mom was incredibly brave to be doing this job as a 22-year-old in the late 1950s. She was new to the big city, having come from a small town where she would have been largely oblivious to criminal elements such as prostitution and illegal booze houses.

I really do believe that Mom was a trailblazer for women in the police force. And although she would have probably gone far in her career, that was not to be. Love and family were to take over her life. The rules in place prevented her from carrying on in this career if she became pregnant or chose to marry another police officer. These rules would change drastically in the following years. Nowadays, husband and wife are not only allowed to stay on the job but also work together. Women who become pregnant are given maternity leave and welcomed back with open arms after the birth of their child.

I imagine she gained so much insight into life in those few years that she served in the Toronto Police Force. I thank her and women like her who were able to pave the way for women around the

The Early Years

world to take on policing roles and rise to the top. I was lucky to have not only my mother to thank but also my grandmother. At a young age, she had been brave enough to cross the ocean not once but twice in order to follow the dream of a new life in a whole new world.

Lesson learned from my grandmother and mother – We all have the choice to bring our dreams to life. We can choose the path we want to follow — like my mother and grandmother did — and decide whether we want to live in fear or find the courage to push through. My mother certainly taught me to chase any dream I wanted and instilled in me the courage to do it.

'Life shrinks or expands in proportion to one's courage.'
~ ANAIS NIN

CHAPTER 4
Lessons From My Father

'My father was my hero, my teacher and the best dad a girl could have.'
~ CAROL COOKE

Dad joined the Toronto Police Force in January 1951 as a clerk then moved into the teletype area. Once he was old enough, he was sent to training to become a police officer and was confirmed a 3rd class PC in February 1955. It wasn't long before he was promoted to a 2nd class PC. In fact, it was only three months. I'm not sure it was because of his prior service and knowledge of the force or if this was common. Two years later, in 1957, he was promoted to a 1st class constable.

It seemed like Dad was destined to be one of the best officers around and always performed his duties, no matter what they were, to the highest standard. One of those times was on 16 December 1957. He was off duty but doing a 'pay duty' — when

The Early Years

companies would hire officers for security or traffic direction — in uniform when he heard what he thought were gun shots and a commotion nearby.

A jeweller named Joseph Bloom who was the owner of Remy Sales had been shot in the right shoulder and pistol-whipped during an attempted robbery. It had taken place on the fifth floor of the Confederation Life Building on Richmond Street East. These types of crimes in the late 50s were not common. After seeing a male run from the scene and throw something into an excavation site, Dad gave chase. He was able to arrest a young man by the name of Benjamin Banack who was 21 at the time, not much younger than himself. A search of the excavation site later revealed a .25 calibre automatic pistol.

Mr Banack had already been serving a four-year sentence for robbery with violence. But after a visit from Queen Elizabeth and Prince Philip, he had been given a reprieve, which had reduced his term and made him eligible for release earlier. He was released just one month before this shooting.

Mr Banack was also charged with the robbery of the Bay Theatre, which had taken place only three days before this attempted robbery. He was subsequently sentenced to 15 years. His defence was that he was 'an abnormal product of war', having spent the entire war in a German prison camp following the invasion of Poland.

Dad was praised for his quick response in chasing down Mr Banack, which put him in a good light with the local detectives. But not one to want to stay a uniform officer, Dad threw himself into learning all he could. With his drive and ambition to be the best police officer that he could be, he continued to challenge himself to learn more about the different units within the job. He thrived on the job and got himself involved in some very diverse and interesting cases and situations. This led him, on 24 May 1958, to take the 'PC's Qualifying Exam for Promotion'. He was bound and determined to move up the ranks.

Lesson — Dream Big, set your goals high, then learn from the bottom up. Always have big dreams, but make sure you have small stepping stones along the way to help you reach that goal. You have to realise that everything you want and dream of doesn't just come to you. It takes hard work and you have to earn your success.

In July 1961, he was appointed a probationary detective. That year the police force started a new area called the Intelligence Bureau, and after an exhaustive search through the department, the powers in that office found that Dad had what they were looking for. They needed someone with great typing and office management systems experience, and with Dad's schooling and background, he was an excellent candidate. He was called into the office and told that they needed someone to devise a complete filing system of organised crime, detailing names, addresses and criminal events throughout Metropolitan Toronto and neighbouring cities. He jumped at the chance to put his skills to use. He set up such a great system that soon he found himself lecturing in the police college to international police forces who wanted to set up similar systems.

Dad was in charge of this area, supervising five staff. For three years, they continuously gathered intelligence through phone wiretaps, file records, tips from the lesser criminals and regular surveillance, even at funerals. The Mafia in Canada were running a booming business through loan-sharking, extortion, prostitution, gambling, bawdyhouses (brothels) and anything else illegal that would turn a fast profit. The system that he devised was so good that they eventually moved it into the digital world. In July 1963, he was promoted to full detective and moved from the Intelligence Bureau to the Break and Enter Squad.

Dad's bosses were so impressed with his rise up the ranks and how well he had worked in his various posts that in September of 1964 he was given a new role. This time, he was appointed as a detective on the Royal Commission inquiring into the circumstances around the Windfall Oils and Mines jump on the Toronto stock exchange. The company's stock had risen from 56 cents to $5.60 and back to 80 cents in July 1965.

This was a huge case in Canada that started in late winter 1964, when Texas Gulf Sulphur geologists working near Timmins, Ontario, found a copper-silver-zinc ore body worth an estimated $2 billion. In July 1965, rumours were circulating in Toronto that this ore body had reached the Windfall Oils and Mines claim, owned by George and Viola MacMillan. It was never proved that the MacMillans had started the rumours, but the scam, which involved massive movement on the stock exchange, temporarily killed off the Toronto Stock Exchange as a global mining financial centre; hence the Ontario Securities Commission asked for a Royal Commission.

The Royal Commission had a huge amount of evidence that needed to be looked at, and as it was being held in Toronto, there were big costs to contend with. The desire to save the taxpayers' money led to a brilliant piece of improvisation by Dad. The question was how to transport the 35 boxes containing the much-discussed Windfall core from Timmins to Toronto without a substantial outlay. The total weight of the core boxes was approximately 1,400 pounds. The cost to transport the core boxes by Air Canada freight , plus insurance, would be about $7,500. Road transportation would be even higher. So, thinking outside the box, he asked Ontario Mines Minister, George Wardrobe, who was in Timmins as a voluntary witness before the commission, whether the Mines Department could help. They did and cost to the commission was nil – therefore a huge savings to the taxpayer.

Lesson — Learn to think outside the square. Too many times we just do what we have been taught to do instead of trying a new and better way. Both my parents were great in teaching me to think more broadly when problems arose. Just because something has been done one way in the past doesn't necessarily mean it should continue to be done the same way. There is never a problem that can't be solved; you just may have to do it differently.

Dad then moved to head up the Morality Bureau, which looked into the gambling issues in the city of Toronto. It was in this unit, four months after starting, that he discovered that six detectives were working illegally with five bookmakers.

He secretly worked out of the Royal Canadian Mounted Police (RCMP) offices and recruited officers he trusted for surveillance and monitoring of wiretaps of the officers doing the wrong thing. After three months of investigating, there were a number of search warrants executed on the bookmakers and the police officers' homes, where evidence of guilt was found. All officers were suspended immediately and went to trial in due course. One officer pled guilty as soon as he could and was sentenced to six months jail; the other five officers were found guilty but appealed to a higher court. Unfortunately, the charges were thrown out due to the RCMP making technical mistakes on their warrants. When he announced his judgment, the Appeal Court judge's statement said, 'It is with regret we dismiss the conviction of these men.' So, these officers were soon back on the job in other locations.

Due to this investigation, the police chief at the time, Chief Adamson, decided that the police force needed a unit to oversee the control over the large staff. In 1976, Dad and Inspector Bill Swanton were asked to set up a new unit called Internal Affairs. I remember this time in our family life as one of Dad being under a lot of stress. He couldn't understand why officers would jeopardise a good paying job to do something underhand and illegal. But his integrity was beyond reproach, and he believed that anyone in this type of work should be the same, which is why he worked so hard in this area.

Lesson — If there is one thing in life that you should have, it is integrity. Dad always taught us that we had to know what our values were in life and live up to them, no matter what.

The Early Years

Dad continued to rise up the ranks of the department, and in early 1979, he was promoted to inspector, then in August 1980 to staff inspector. After this promotion, he was asked to head up the Intelligence Bureau, which was where he had originally started in 1961 with only five staff. He was heading back to head up a unit that now comprised 134 members dealing with organised crime. But his time in this unit was not without controversy. There were quite a few times when his work did affect our family, especially when he received threats due to his involvement with a number of cases.

One in particular was the very controversial 'Bathhouse Raids' in 1981. Dad told me that information had been obtained that gay bathhouses were being controlled by organised crime gangs based in the United States. But the media and people within the gay community were saying it was all about homophobia and a deliberate attempt by police to silence the gay community and their activism in the city of Toronto.

At this time, the gay community was just starting to emerge in Toronto, and they had men's clubs throughout the city. The four that were targeted in this operation, 'Operation Soap', were the Club Baths, the Romans II Health and Recreation Spa, the Richmond Street Health Emporium and the Barracks.

Dad had organised undercover officers to frequent the bathhouses for about four months to gain information about how the clubs were organised, where the money was sent and what exactly was going on inside, such as whether there was prostitution happening.

The raids were conducted on the four major bathhouses in Toronto, all done at the same time on one day. There was uproar in the city with the gay community protesting through the streets of downtown Toronto and numerous media outlets calling for the resignation of the then chief, Jack Ackroyd.

That night, the highest number of people were arrested in one night in Toronto, over 250 men. There were a number of drug charges laid, but those who owned or worked in the bathhouses were charged with 'keeping a common bawdyhouse' and patrons were charged with being 'found in a common bawdyhouse'. A majority of the charges were either dismissed or dropped.

There was a lot of damage done at the premises. Dad told me that the damage was done by people found in there trying to run out, but information found says that the damage was caused by police. Looking at the footage taken of the damage, it certainly looks as if it was caused by police, but nothing came of the allegations.

There were calls for an independent inquiry, which never happened, but the raids galvanised the gay community and its allies. This was transformative for how the LGBTQ community was treated in the city of Toronto and in Canada. Some even said that in hindsight the raids were probably one of the best things that ever happened to the LGBTQ community at that time.

I can say that it was certainly a stressful time in our family. Even though Dad tried not to bring work home, it was in all the papers, on all radio and across the television news. I could comment on the raids in hindsight, but that wouldn't be fair. Dad thought he was doing the right thing at the time due to his belief that there was criminal activity happening within these clubs, and although there were few convictions, that is the way the law works. Dad always said that he was there to enforce the laws, that the police are not always right, and the courts are there to make that decision.

In 2016, the Chief of Police, Mark Saunders, publicly apologised to the city's LGBTQ community as the first step in improving the police force's relationships with the community throughout Canada's largest city.

The Early Years

There are many more stories that came from Dad's time in Intelligence, but that could be a book in itself. Suffice to say, there were many investigations into organised crime by Mafia and bike gangs, such as kidnapping, money laundering and murder for hire, and a number of lives were saved due to the work of his unit.

Lesson — Have moral courage. Always do what you believe is the right thing, even if many are against you. Dad always taught us to come to our own conclusions, stay strong to what we believed in. He thought that even if you disagreed with someone, you could still love them.

In May of 1983, Dad was promoted to superintendent and transferred to 55 Division, where I had just started my career as an officer. Needless to say, I had to go elsewhere as I wasn't allowed to work directly for my father, so I was transferred to 54 Division, which bordered 55 Division.

Dad only stayed at 55 for just over a year but while there showed the men and women who worked for him that he wasn't just a sit-behind-the-desk kind of man. He regularly went out with another officer in his car, driving around the area, even stopping people if he thought they were up to no good. He wanted his men and women to follow his lead and not just take verbal directions from him.

Lesson — Don't ask people to do things that you wouldn't do yourself.

Only a year later, he was promoted to staff superintendent and was transferred to Public Affairs, an office that was situated at police headquarters. His new duties included being the media liaison for the force, overseeing visitation of dignitaries and the new museum. He remarked to me once that this was probably the most stressful job he had during his time on the force. Dealing with the media meant he had to be extremely careful in how he answered their questions. At times, he would take ten to fifteen minutes to explain something, but the media would only report one to two minutes. Other times, his comments would be taken out of context. So, he chose his words wisely and learned who he could trust to report honestly.

While in this position, one of his most passionate jobs was revamping the Police Museum. He wanted to bring it into the 20th century by modernising it with computers and interactive areas for people to learn more about the history of the force. He looked for sponsors to assist with the purchase of historical items, such as the 1913 Ford paddy wagon. Through contacts he had made on the job, Dad was able to get Imperial Oil to donate the money for the purchase. Since then, the museum has been constantly updated. Today, it is viewed by many as one of the best police history collections and is a great source on the history of crime in Toronto.

Dad was also honoured to be in charge of a number of visits from dignitaries, such as Pope John Paul II and the Queen Mother, the latter of whom he had a private audience with. He described the Queen Mother as 'a very petite and engaging woman' who, once she found out he was of Scottish decent, made him feel like family. When we asked what they had talked about, he remained very discreet, even with us. He would only tell us that they had talked about where his father was from, but nothing else. He had been with her for over 20 minutes, so I am sure they spoke about more than that.

A major incident that he had to deal with involved a terrorist group that called itself the 'Armenian Secret Army for the Liberation of Our Homeland'. The group demanded the release of three Armenians prisoners who had been charged with murder in connection to a siege at the Turkish Embassy in Ottawa. They threatened to bomb the tracks of the Toronto subway system on 1 April 1985 unless their demands were met.

The decision by Chief Jack Marks to let the public know of this threat meant that Dad had to work non-stop over the weekend.

The Early Years

Some people thought it was an April Fools prank, but all the officials were taking it seriously, and Dad was dealing with the media constantly. There turned out to be no bombs or devices planted, but this was only confirmed after thousands of police, security agents and dogs combed the tracks and tunnels of the subway system, patrolled the buses, subway cars and carried out spot checks of passengers carrying packages.

Toronto Transit Commission Chairman Julian Porter and a number of city officials criticised Chief Marks for releasing the information to the public. Dad had to deal with the ensuing controversy from a media perspective.

One of his last duties in this role was to organise the International Chiefs of Police Conference in 1987. With 6,000 officers from around the world attending, it was a massive undertaking with a budget of $130,000. This wasn't a huge sum to be able to pull this off, but again, his contacts through his years on the job came in handy. He approached the Royal Canadian Mounted Police (RCMP) to see if they would perform for free their Musical Ride and pipe band as well as other police force pipe bands to put together a 'band tattoo' as entertainment.

Once these bands were all confirmed, he approached the City of Toronto to acquire the Coliseum at the Canadian National Exhibition ground. He was able to secure vehicles from Chrysler, General Motors and Ford to transport the delegates from their hotels to the conference. He also managed to get a local businessman who was in the meat-packing industry to donate the many thousands of pounds of beef for the closing dinner.

In the end, the conference was a huge success, and he even came in under budget by $5,000. Needless to say, the city and the chief of police at the time, Jack Marks, were very happy.

He had enjoyed his time in Public Affairs and had become a 'jack of all trades'; however, once the conference was finished, Dad decided that he had had enough of this position. He asked the chief to let him go back to working with the men and women on the street, back into what he described as 'real policing'.

Lesson — Don't be scared of change. If you are not happy doing the job you are in, then do something else. Amazing opportunities can come from change.

In March 1988, Dad was transferred to 1 District Headquarters as the commander. He was now in charge of a huge area comprising the entire west end of Toronto, which included four divisions, 1,200 personnel and a budget in excess of $2.5 million per year. Dad was back where he loved being, dealing with the men and women of the force. He loved his time there, even though it was a big commute each day from the east end of Toronto to the west end. However, his time there wasn't without controversy, and that came when one of his officers, Constable David Deviney, shot and killed a man by the name of Lester Donaldson.

Lester Donaldson was shot in the chest after Deviney and four others said that he had lunged at them with a knife. Back in those days, these types of incidents were investigated by police themselves, and at the onset, Deviney was cleared of any wrongdoing. But there was a huge outcry in the community, with calls of racism due to the fact that Lester Donaldson was black and had schizophrenia.

The newspapers were filled with stories looking at the Black community's perception of the incident with allegations that race was a motivating factor in the shooting. Tensions were so high that it was decided that the Ontario Provincial Police would be called in to investigate and Deviney was charged with manslaughter. Once the charge was laid, approximately 2,500 officers took to the street to protest, with Dad supporting them and claiming that the charge had only been laid as a political response to the vocal Black community.

Dad had spoken without the consent of the force and was called before the chief to explain himself. He did not waiver in his support for his officers. However, the incident sparked racial tensions between the police and the community that hadn't ever been seen before in Toronto.

Deviney was later acquitted by a jury, but because of the protests and the subsequent inquest into Donaldson's death, a task force was formed. Justice Clare Lewis, who led it, recommended the formation of the Ontario Special Investigations Unit in order to independently investigate officer-involved fatalities and serious injuries. The unit is still in operation today, and new training for officers in regard to de-escalation was put in place.

Dad clearly felt that he was doing the right thing at the time, but I sometimes wonder whether his feelings towards how he handled the situation would be different if he were alive today.

Lesson — It is important to look at situations from all points of view. Just because you have one belief doesn't mean that you are right.

In February 1990, after missing out on a deputy chief promotion and with 39 years' service to the city of Toronto, Dad decided that it was time to retire. He had been diagnosed with macular degeneration, which meant he was losing his eyesight. Besides, at 55 years old, he wanted to spend time with Mom and enjoy life.

He was often described as someone who helped pave the way for a new generation of police officers and, at the end of his career, was very supportive of new Chief William McCormack's emphasis on community-based policing. Numerous times over the years I have heard people remembering him as giving public support of his officers and as a person with a great deal of moral courage. He wasn't a perfect man, but he always owned up to his mistakes.

He believed in constant learning and, throughout his career, continued to take courses not only through universities but elsewhere too. On one occasion, he went to a Catholic silent retreat for a weekend, even though he wasn't Catholic. He knew that no matter where you were, you could learn and take something good out of it.

He was dedicated, proud and committed to serving his community. He served under six police chiefs, and on his retirement, he stated that he believed his father would be proud of him. He praised those officers who had worked with him and for him, saying that he cherished their comradeship, their thoroughness and their dedication and thanked them for making him look good!

He was a selfless man who always wanted to give to others. No matter what, if someone was in need, he was there. He didn't look for praise or thanks but just wanted to make life better for others and did good deeds without wanting anything in return. This way of life continued until dementia and blindness took over and he left this world on 21 March 2016, at the age of 82.

Lesson — Take care of yourself but always give of yourself to others. Don't look for praise or accolades but find happiness in the giving of yourself.

PART 2
Family And Career

CHAPTER 5
Family Life Lessons

'Families are the compass that guides us.
They are the inspiration to reach great heights, and our
comfort when we occasionally falter.'
~ BRAD HENRY

Mom and Dad met on the job, but at the time they met, the rules of the police force were that you couldn't date anyone, let alone get married to them. This was something that Dad understood but that Mom didn't know at the beginning.

Mom had been working at the 'cattle crossing' directing traffic, but on the day that she met Dad, she had an issue with her foot. As she was unable to stand for long periods of time, she had been directed to do paperwork in the detective office at Court Street Station. While there, she came across a ledger on which were all the officers' names and whether they were single, married or divorced.

Family And Career

She had seen this good-looking young uniform officer a number of times around the station and had found out that his name was Don Banks. So she decided to check the ledger to see if he was married or not. Next to his name, it said that he was divorced. She had never spoken to him, but that day, he happened to come into the detective office to do some work and they got talking.

During their conversation, Dad asked Mom if she had any sisters. She told him that she had three, at which point he asked if any of them were good-looking. She thought to herself, 'You cheeky bugger!' but said, 'As a matter of fact, I live with one of them, and yes, she is a nice-looking woman.' She asked him whether he would like to come for dinner and meet her, adding that her name was Rheta. He agreed.

Mom wasn't too happy that he wanted to meet her sister, but at the time, she had no idea about the police force dating rules, whereas Dad did. She asked him what his favourite dinner was, and the answer came, 'Spare ribs.' So, she rushed home after work and organised the dinner.

Dad met Rheta at dinner, but there was no spark. However, for my mom, it was 'love at first sight'. Shortly after this dinner, Mom and Rheta went on a week's holiday to New York City, where she said she pined for Dad the whole time. She told Rheta that she was going to marry him one day.

Once she was back from her holiday, Phyllis invited Don for dinner with not only Rheta but also their friend Lorna. She had the entire dinner prepared, but he didn't show up. He called her to apologise, explaining that he was on a case and still at work. Once he had finished work, he would come and take her out to dinner, he told her. So, while Rheta and Lorna ate, Phyllis waited. It was fairly late when Don arrived, but he took her over to Bathurst and Bloor Streets to a restaurant called the Candlelight café. That was the start of their relationship.

The relationship continued to bloom, albeit quietly, to hide it from the police force. They were both still working at the Court Street Station, and it was extremely hard to keep their secret, so they wouldn't speak or look at each other while there.

At Christmas in 1959, Phyllis finally took Don up to Smooth Rock Falls to meet her parents. It would have been very scary for Don to face her mom, Elizabeth. Although she was a wonderful woman, my grandmother was a tough lady and would have been very protective of her daughter. He would have had to prove he was worthy of Phyllis, especially because they lived so far away. But he brought gifts for Christmas, and he had bought a beautiful big bulky knit white sweater for Phyllis, which she loved. The meeting with her parents went very well, which helped the relationship between them even more. Don could be a bit of a smooth talker, and I have no doubt that Phyllis' parents were smitten with this young man their youngest daughter had brought home for Christmas.

In early 1960, Dad ended up in hospital with a hernia so Mom went to visit him on her lunch break. While there, he confessed that he had been dating a couple of other women at the same time, but he looked at her and thanked her for coming to visit, stating that she was the only one who had taken the time to visit him. It was then that she also found out that the beautiful white sweater he had bought, he had also given the same to two others. His Scottish blood had prompted him to buy three sweaters after getting a 'policeman's discount' in the garment district of Toronto. Although Phyllis was shocked, she forgave him, continued to date him and he, exclusively, her.

In June 1960, Don took Phyllis to the Candlelight Cafe where he proposed. She said yes. Neither of them knew that as officers they weren't allowed to marry and both remain on the force. They knew that they weren't supposed to be dating but thought that marriage would be considered different, especially if they were put in different areas of the city. When they did find out they

Family And Career

couldn't both stay on the job, they decided to go right to the top and made an appointment with the chief of police, Chief Mackey. This is what he said: 'I'm sorry you aren't allowed. There is nothing I can do; those are the rules.'

Phyllis was disappointed. She had enjoyed her two years on the force, and being forced to quit after such a short time felt like a waste of her training. Nonetheless, they decided that she would quit while Don continued his career on the police force.

Soon after, my parents had an opportunity to rent a house which prompted them to quickly get married. The house, in the Toronto Beaches area, belonged to Dad's former in-laws, with whom he had stayed close since his divorce. On 10 September 1960, they became Mr and Mrs Donald Banks.

Dad continued his career and Mom wasn't worried about getting work. She decided not to go back to teaching right away; instead, she got a job at a bank at Woodbine Avenue and Gerrard Avenue East. It wasn't too long before she was pregnant with her first child, me.

We lived as a small new family in that house until the spring of 1963 when Mom and Dad decided that they wanted to buy their own home. There was an area in the east of Toronto, in the newly formed leafy suburb of Scarborough, that was being built called Guildwood Village. That is where they bought their first home together.

It was a white brick house with a lovely porch across the front. Mom, with her love of gardening learned from her father, planted beautiful flowers in boxes across the front.

It was the home they would live in for the next 41 years. This is also the house where the family welcomed their second child, Cynthia Lee, or Cindy as she was to be known, on 1 July 1963. We were also lucky enough to have a beautiful dog enter our lives, Casey, a black Lab cross Cocker Spaniel and the family was complete.

Lesson — Sometimes rules can't be broken.

CHAPTER 6
Sisters Are Forever

*'When you have a sister, you never truly forget the past.
If you do, she'll be happy to remind you of all
your stupidest mistakes.'*
~ KATE MILLER-WILSON

I believe I was born pig-headed and stubborn with a determined spirit. Right from the beginning, I was always taught to stand up for myself and question things. One of the earliest memories I can recall was being scolded with a slap on the bottom and sent to my room. Once there, I had a meltdown pulling the drawers of my dresser out, emptying all that was inside, then lying on the floor kicking the bedroom door, pounding the floor and screaming.

Once I had got this out of my system (or maybe I just got tired of the antics), I was somehow able to open the door, head down the hallway, sliding down the stairs to the basement on my bum where I found Mom in the laundry room. With a defiant stance and hands on my hips, I looked at Mom and stated, 'That didn't hurt.' I remember just standing there almost egging her on. What she did or didn't say to me in the moments that followed, I don't remember, but I do remember being spanked again, taken upstairs, put in my room, and made to stay there.

What I did learn that day was respect, never to speak back to my mother and take whatever punishment came my way — not that there was a lot of punishment in our family. In later years, I asked my mother if she remembered this incident, and she was surprised to hear that I did. It had happened just before my sister was born, so I would have been just under two years of age.

As sisters, Cindy and I were close, but growing up, I don't think we were 'best' friends. We each had our own lives, interests and our own friends. I probably wasn't the nicest of sisters in our younger years. There were times when I blamed Cindy for things that I had done wrong. Cindy was a quiet child and I was the loud one. I'm not sure if this was me just being the eldest, bossy one. There are times now that I look back and think about how mean I was to her, but she just seemed to take everything in her stride.

Mom and Dad had taken in a boarder when I was about five years old, a university student who rented a room from us. We were told that this was strictly his room, and under no circumstances were we to venture into his room. He had the most amazing map of the world on his wall above a desk, which I was always intrigued by.

One day while he was out of the house and Mom was busy with household duties, I took Cindy by the hand and led her into the forbidden territory. With a red crayon in hand, I helped Cindy climb up on the desk, put the crayon in her hand and asked her if she wanted to go on a trip. With the nod of her head, I placed her hand and crayon on the map.

'This is where we live. Let's go here,' I told her, pointing to the other side of the map.

I moved her hand, with the crayon in it, to the other side of the map. This continued for several trips, so that the beautiful map had red lines running across and up and down. Cindy became bored with the game. I helped her climb down from the desk, and we left the room, all completely unknown to our mom.

It was a few hours later, when our boarder came home, entered his room and let out a very loud yell, that our 'trips' were discovered. We were called into the living room and told to sit on the couch. Dad asked us who had done this dastardly deed, but as we sat there, not a word came out of Cindy.

'Well, I don't like to tattle,' I started, 'but I saw Cindy going in the room with a red crayon and told her not to.'

There were no other questions asked. Cindy was scolded and sent to our room. I don't know if Dad actually knew I had been the instigator, but if he had really thought about it, he might have found it strange that I knew the colour of the crayon that had been used to mark the map. Besides, how could Cindy, at three years old, climb on the desk by herself? I do know that it cost Mom and Dad a lot of money to have that map replaced.

I was in grade 1 and six years old when I first heard the word 'Fuck'. I had no idea what it meant, but I knew it was bad. Once home, I wrote that word on the white brick wall of our house under the carport, with a blue crayon this time. After feeling very satisfied with my artwork, I went inside and forgot about it. That was until Dad pulled his car into the driveway and under the carport. As he got out of the car, he let out one heck of a yell, which could probably have been heard down the street! He came in the door extremely angry. In 1967, this was not a word that was regularly used, and any kind of swearing was not heard in our household. It wasn't until we were much older that we would here the occasional 'shit' used by our parents.

Dad called us to the couch in the living room and asked who had written on the wall outside. Cindy was again very quiet;

she knew nothing of what I had done. She just sat there with a look of surprise on her face, as I again blamed her. Cindy took the punishment in her stride, not saying anything in her defence. Now, if Mom and Dad had thought about it, Cindy was four and would have no idea how to even spell the word 'fuck' and had probably never even heard it. Now I sound like a bad child, and I probably was for a year or two around that time, but I would have fought to the death for her if she had needed me to be in her corner.

Cindy and I were the only two girls on our street for most of our younger years, so we played with the local neighbourhood boys. This involved playing tag, baseball, road hockey in the summer, ice hockey in the winter, building snow forts, having snowball fights or skating on the rink Dad had made in the backyard. Sometimes we would even get the boys to hold an end of our skipping rope or jumpsy elastic (rubber bands attached together we jumped over at different heights). It was surprising how accommodating the boys could be!

We were always outside, no matter the weather, and would only show up when our hunger got to us. And we were never at home on the weekends. This is where our parents really trusted us and taught us independence, although as we moved into our teenage years, I am sure we tested the trust they had for us at times. But we always seemed to get through whatever was thrown before us, and our love as a family was always what kept us grounded.

Mom had enrolled us in Saturday dance classes. You name it, we took it: ballet, tap, baton twirling and acrobats. I remember loving acrobats, which eventually led to gymnastics. At our primary school, from almost day one of kindergarten, I was showing off doing cartwheels and the splits. The principal of our school, Mr Orrett, was the gymnastics coach, and as soon as he saw me showing off, he fast-tracked me into the gym to take part in the gymnastics team. I was definitely the only kinder student there!

But I loved it. I wanted to practise all the time, and for the next five years, all I wanted to do was be a gymnast.

Cindy loved gymnastics too. It was the one thing that we loved doing together in the backyard. It was the start of our love of sport although Cindy became the star basketball and volleyball player and track and field athlete, while eventually I became a swimmer. I am not sure how Mom did it, between getting me to swim meets, getting Cindy to basketball games and making sure she was watching us compete as much as possible.

We were never allowed to watch television on a weeknight except for Friday nights and Sundays to watch The Wonderful World of Disney. Weeknights were all about sport training, practising the piano, homework or time with the family.

Guildwood Village was a wonderful place to grow up; it was our world. After attending Popular Road Public School until grade 6, we then went down the street and around the corner to Jack Minor Senior Public School for grades 7 and 8, then about a kilometre away to Sir Wilfred Laurier Collegiate Institute for high school. So, we really never ventured far from home unless it was for sport or to visit family.

As Cindy and I got older, we grew closer and became friends. We were both moving on with our own lives. I joined the police force, while Cindy went to university for a degree in Radio/Television Production, fell in love, got married and started a family.

We have become best of friends, and there is nothing I wouldn't do for her. I'm just glad that she has forgiven me for all the terrible things I put her through in our much younger years. At least, I think she has forgiven me! The one thing I will always regret was not being around for her when her marriage was falling apart. I could only help from afar.

We really did have the ideal little family. Mom stayed home with us until we were old enough to attend school. Once we were in school, she decided that she wanted to go back to work. I remember in the early years of Mom's return to teaching, Dad was

Family And Career

working in the Break and Enter Squad. The two of them really did sacrifice their own relationship for the sake of us girls.

Dad worked a permanent type of night shift, 7 pm to 3 am, or 8 pm to 4 am, would come home and go to bed, while Mom would get us up and ready for school. We only had to go across the street for primary school, then Mom would head to her school to teach. Cindy and I would come home for lunch when Dad would be up and waiting for us. After school, we would head home to see Dad preparing dinner. Mom would arrive home, we would all have dinner together, and Dad would head to work for the night. This cycle of life went on for several years, but Mom and Dad's love for each other and their family never waned; it just grew stronger. I'm sure there were tough times for both of them, but they never let us see those times.

Lesson — This taught me that the power of love, with the willingness to each sacrifice just a little, can get you through any problems in life.

> *'Love is not a feeling of happiness.*
> *Love is a willingness to sacrifice.'*
> ~ MICHAEL NOVAK

One important thing that Mom and Dad did do for us was buy a cottage in Northern Ontario when we were young children. Mom's parents had moved from Smooth Rock Falls to Cardiff, Ontario, and on one of our many visits to them, they made the decision to buy a tiny cottage on Paudash Lake, which was nearby. This was where we could spend time as a family during the summer months. It was where Mom and Dad had time together as a couple and where I believe our bond as a family came from. Two days after school finished in June, we were packed into our car and taken up to the cottage to spend two months, our summer holidays, until about two days before school began again in September. Of course, Dad couldn't stay there the whole time, but most of his holidays were kept until summer so he could be with us.

It was an idyllic life as a kid, with a lake and bushland to play in. Our summers were spent barefoot in bathing suits. The cottage was where we learned to swim, waterski, drive a boat, build imagination and where first loves were born and lost to tears. It certainly was a kid's paradise. There were no such things as home computers, mobile phones or console games. These months really made us use our imaginations and whatever was in nature to create our fun. It was where I learned the true meaning of family.

We got to know our grandparents and learn from them as well. Grandpa instilled in us a love of the outdoors and gardening, just as he had done with his own children. Grandma, always the generous cook, fed us to our hearts content. I can still smell the homemade bread as she pulled it from the oven and taste the meals she made with produce from Grandpa's garden.

It was also the place where I first experienced the death of someone I loved. It had such a profound impact on me; I remember it clearly. It was 11 days after my sister's 11th birthday, in July 1974. Cindy and I were playing in the sandpit — we would spend hours there creating other worlds — when my mother's father pulled into the driveway. He was walking towards the back door of the cottage when he spoke.

'Get in the cottage, girls,' he said gruffly. 'Your grandfather died.'

'You're not dead,' I replied with a little laugh.

'Not me, your other grandfather,' he said, his voice angrier. 'Now, get in the house.'

I was stunned because no one in my family was ever supposed to die, and I just couldn't understand not ever seeing him again.

It was also the first time I ever saw my father cry. My dad, the huge, tough cop was crying. At that point, I thought the world had turned upside down and everything was not as it was supposed to be. That was the moment when I realised that not even my dad was a superhero! I don't remember my grandfather's funeral even though I know we went. I do remember coming to terms with the fact that life does not go on forever.

This was the start of my belief that life is there to be lived because you never know how long you have.

'Perhaps they are not the stars, but rather openings in Heaven where the love of our lost ones pours through and shines down upon us to let us know they are happy.'
~ UNKNOWN

CHAPTER 7
Doing Things Differently

*'There is no greater disability in society than the
inability to see a person as more.'*
~ ROBERT M. HENSEL

The cottage was a significant place in our lives. After massive renovations, it became a retirement home for Mom and Dad until it was too hard to stay there during the winter months, and it eventually was sold. I had always thought that it would be around forever and believed that, one day, Cindy and I would be taking our own children to 'the cottage', but life has a funny way of changing direction.

The cottage was also where, around 1972, Cindy and I learned the fact that we had a half-brother, Brian. Dad took us out in the boat on the pretext of just having a ride. In the middle of the lake, he stopped the engine. He then looked at us seriously and said, 'I just wanted to come out here and tell you that you have a brother.'

Family And Career

No lead-up to it, just matter of fact. We both laughed and said, 'No, we don't.' Dad went on to explain that he had been married before he met our mother and that Brian had been born from that marriage. When I asked why he hadn't told us earlier, he explained that Brian had some health issues and he didn't think we would have understood at a younger age. He told us that Down syndrome was a genetic disorder, that Brian looked a little different and had an intellectual disability but that, when we met him, we shouldn't treat him any different than if we were meeting a new friend.

To this day, I'm not sure why he told us in the boat. Maybe he thought we would try to run away from him. But once we found out, I was looking forward to meeting Brian and having a brother. It was about a year before this would happen. Brian became part of our family, coming for visits by train from the other side of the city. He became a part of our lives.

Brian loved the fact that there were police officers in the family, and on one trip to visit us, we took him to 5 District Traffic, where Dad had been working. The guys on shift that day were fabulous, put him in the sidecar of a motorcycle and drove him around the back parking lot. He was presented with an old police hat and a memo book. That night, back at home for dinner, he wouldn't take that hat off and scribbled in his memo book about all the 'bad' things we were doing. He possibly took his 'policing' a bit far. After returning to his mother's house, he went around the neighbourhood knocking on doors, asking if they had called the police. With his hat on his head and notebook in hand, he was ready to take a report. Luckily, Brian was very well known around the neighbourhood, and people just played along with him. I honestly think that if Brian hadn't been born with Down syndrome he would have followed in the policing line of work.

Brian was an amazing person who, despite having Down syndrome, worked three jobs, eventually had a girlfriend and, for a time, was able to live in his own apartment. He worked at his church as a cleaner and at the YMCA handing out towels and locker keys. He also got involved learning how to take photos for an opera company. He taught me that there is no such thing as disability, only ability.

Brian would always take the GO train from the west end of the city to the east where we lived. He always brought a number of bags with him full of his 'treasures'. He had a huge personality and a loud voice; everything about Brian was 'big'. As Cindy would say, 'He had a big personality, big voice, big social life, big passions, big enthusiasm, big dislikes, big family and big bags.' I remember times where he would get off the train carrying his possessions. But there was also a time where he didn't get off the train at all. As it was pulling slowly out of the station, I was frantically waving at the train conductor. They had to stop the train to find him. He had his headphones on, listening to his music and in a completely different world! A tap on the shoulder and he grabbed his big bags, got off the train, didn't say a word to the conductor, or me for that matter, and walked towards the exit. It was at the exit that he finally acknowledged me, and I got a hug!

On one particular visit, Cindy picked him up from the train and made the trip to Don and Phyllis' cottage on Paudash Lake. I was already there, and we made plans to head by boat to the local pub on the lake for dinner, just the three of us. The pub was packed with a live country band playing, which was Brian's favourite type of music, and there was a lot of dancing. It was certainly a night to remember.

Cindy describes it further: 'There was a lot of dancing – even in between tables. At one point, I had to rest my dancing feet and sit down, but Brian, the energizer bunny, outlasted me. I remember glancing over my right shoulder and seeing him with a bottle of beer raised high in one hand, while he conducted the band with the other, multi-tasking as he danced and sang with a group of ladies who were lovin' him. Then he plopped himself down beside me, gestured to one of the ladies dancing right beside us and said, 'Nice legs.' And like this 'leg man' often did, he repeated this statement over and over — until he was certain the lady with the legs knew she had an admirer. It didn't take long for Brian to dance with every dancing woman in that pub. Now we all know that this kind of 'high' can't last forever, but the plunge seemed to happen so fast — I mean I wasn't counting his drinks. All of a sudden, Brian, with glazed eyes, was boasting to the room "me drunk, me drunk".'

It was time to, somehow, get him home. We did manage to get him in the boat. Cindy was driving like a crazy woman, while I was trying to hold on to Brian as he stood in the boat punching the air yelling 'me drunk, me drunk'. We managed to get him back to the cottage and up to bed without too much fuss, just hoping that he wouldn't be sick as his words changed to 'me sick, me sick'. The next morning, he came down to breakfast announcing to everyone 'me drunk, me sick' over and over. As Cindy and I were to learn, there were no secrets with Brian.

In the early 90s, I introduced Brian to an officer who I was working with, Detective Bill Soules. Bill was an amazing man who took to Brian and Brian to him. Bill had a boat moored at the Scarborough Bluffs Yacht Club and invited us out for a fishing trip. I think this was one of the best days of Brian's life. Bill taught him how to drive the boat, how to fish, clean the fish and even cook it so we could all feast on it once back on dry land. It was a long day and one that Brian wished would not end. I remember taking him to the train to head home and hoping he wouldn't fall asleep on the train and miss his stop! Once I headed home, I called his mom, Adele, to let her know he was on the train and told her about his day. She stopped me after I had said that Brian had cooked his own fish and had a feast and said, 'But Brian hates fish. I can't believe he ate it!' I replied, 'Well, he might hate fish, but he caught it himself!'

This one-day trip with Bill led Brian to constantly call him at work to say hi and ask when they could go out fishing again. Unfortunately, this didn't happen, but Brian never forgot that day.

Later in life, Mom and Dad had to stop Brian's visits to them because Brian would sometimes become belligerent, angry and physical. Dad wouldn't be able to handle him due to Brian's physical strength. I didn't see him for several years due to moving to Australia, but Cindy continued to see him and have contact.

Brian was then diagnosed with Alzheimer's and eventually put into care. He passed away peacefully on 26 September 2012, at the young age of 56, leaving behind lessons for so many people on what it means to live with Down syndrome or a disability. From the day he was born, people underestimated what his life would be like, doubting if he could even have a life. But he defied everyone, holding down three jobs and eventually even living on his own and having a girlfriend. There is even a stained-glass window in his memory at his church, which he was involved with for 52 years of his life.

I never saw the 'disability' of Down syndrome in Brian. To me, he will always remain that man with the huge personality with a big voice, dancing between the tables and eating the fish that he caught!

Brian taught me a huge lesson, one that I would take with me into my introduction to disability years later: you can accomplish anything, but you might have to do things a bit differently.

CHAPTER 8

My Own Learning Begins

'Until you step into the unknown, you don't know what you're made of.'
~ ROY T. BENNETT

As a little girl of about four, I used to sit on my dad's knee, mesmerised by a special wallet that he carried. It had a very shiny badge on one side with his picture on the other side. It was a policeman's badge. At that age, my dad seemed like a really big man to me, a giant of a man, and even though I probably didn't understand it at the time, I was very proud of him and of his job.

I learned very early on in life that the shiny badge gave him some sort of authority. But it wasn't until I began hearing stories of life as a police officer that I grasped what that job entailed. At home,

Family And Career

police officers would be coming and going as all of Dad's friends were in the same job. Mom and Dad's social life revolved around all those men and their wives.

As I grew, I realised that policing was a part of our family. It felt like the whole family was involved. And even though I was proud of what my family did, I swore I would never follow in Dad's footsteps, or Mom's for that matter, as we had enough officers splattered throughout our family. I was the typical kid who changed my mind every year as to what I wanted to do when I 'grew up'. One year a doctor, one year a teacher and one year even a cartographer.

I wasn't sure what I wanted to do when I finished high school; I just knew that I didn't want to be a police officer because there were too many in the family already. But when high school finished and I was a bit over studying, I decided that I needed a job. Other than working in the food industry though, I really didn't know what I could do. These next couple of years taught me many lessons.

I'm not sure how it happened, but I applied for a job with the Toronto Police Force as a clerk, and on 18 November 1980, I was sworn in as an employee. I started out in the RIB Unit (Records Information Bureau). This was well before the computer systems that held data on anyone the police might stop and question. Instead, the information obtained by officers was written on cards that were stored in trays in a large machine that we would sit at. The cards were kept in alphabetical order, and when officers on the road needed information, we would get a call to look up if the offender had been stopped in the past. Talk about antiquated. It is amazing to think I was part of that system and around to see the computer age take hold!

In the Records Bureau office, there was also an area where specialised offices like the Hold Up Squad, Homicide Squad or Criminal Investigative Bureau (CIB) would call us to report on a major crime, incident or arrest. We would write it up for distribution to the Headquarters Duty Desk who would then distribute the information to the press. It was an interesting job as we would see all the major incidents that had happened in the city of Toronto. For me, coming right out of high school and being just 18 years old, it was an eye-opening experience, with insight into the criminal workings of a big city. It was interesting to speak with the officers who called but also to hear about what was going on around our city, despite it usually being bad for the people involved.

Even though I grew up within a policing family, I think it was here that my thirst for policing really began. This initial experience gave me an insight as to how the police department worked and gave me the impetus to join 'the job'. That insight along with all the stories that Dad told me while I was growing helped me make the decision.

Typing up the media releases, I started to think that, if I joined the job as an officer, I would be able to make a difference in the world. The problem was I was only 18 and you couldn't become a police officer until the age of 21. But I did know that there was always the possibility of becoming a cadet. Cadet duties had changed since my dad had first joined, so I looked into it and thought it would be a good avenue for me to take.

Cadets were people under 21 who basically did all the joe jobs that no one else really wanted. You also could not carry a gun until you were 21, but it was a good stepping stone.

When I filled out my application, I decided not to tell my parents. My mom would have gone nuts as the job was much different from when she was on the force. As for my dad, I kept it from him as I didn't want any special treatment or fast-tracking.

What I didn't know at the time was that all applications for jobs on the force went through the Intelligence Unit to check for any links to organised crime. Guess who happened to be in charge of that unit when I decided to apply? Yes, my dad! So, when my application arrived in his department, one of his staff members brought it to him right away. I was working day shift that day, at RIB, when I received a phone call from my dad. At first, I thought that something must be terribly wrong because he never called me at work. After saying hello, he asked in almost a frightened tone, 'Are you sure you want to do this? First your mom is going to kill you, and then she will want to kill me because she will think I put you up to this.' I laughed and told him I would stick up for him. I know that secretly Dad was extremely chuffed that a child of his was following in his footsteps, just like he had followed in his father's. Mom did fly off the handle a little, but she was eventually supportive of the direction my life was about to take.

Lesson — It's probably best to be upfront and honest from the start because everyone will find out anyhow! No matter what you are doing, if you are open and honest from the start, it makes things much easier to attain. You could even gain some help by letting others know what you are doing.

I thought that working as a cadet would give me a sense of what the job was like … not much of a sense but a little bit. So, after some minimal training, I started as a cadet at the ripe old age of 19, working at 52 Division on Dundas Street West, right in the downtown core of Toronto. Not only did we cover the Central Business District but also Chinatown on the west to Spading Avenue, Yonge Street on the East, Lake Ontario on the south and up to Bloor Street West on the North. Not a huge area but a very busy one! So talk about getting thrown in the deep end! Most of the work I did was manning the front desk of the station and dealing with people walking in off the street. Sometimes it was taking a report of something that had happened, giving someone directions or directing someone to speak with an officer. It certainly taught me how to speak to people, and it made me learn the city area in order to give directions to people. The odd time I even got out in a car, but only to pick things up for the station, and sometimes this got me into a little bit of hot water.

My Own Learning Begins

It was near the beginning of my career at 52 when I was asked to go out and pick up the staff sergeant and sergeant's lunches. They had ordered food from a local place on Yonge Street. I was given directions and told to pick the food up and come right back. Now I was taught during cadet training that any time I was in the car I was to inform the dispatcher of where I was going and why. However, the staff sergeant in charge, Clarke Winter, forgot to tell me that I didn't have to tell the dispatcher that I was picking up their food! So, like a good little cadet, I got in the unmarked police car and was really excited. It was the first time I had been out on my own, so I diligently called the dispatcher …

Me: 'Dispatcher, this is Cadet 52.'

Dispatcher: 'Yes, Cadet 52, how can I help?'

Me: 'Well, Dispatcher, I am headed to (address) to pick up the boss's lunch.'

Dispatcher: (short pause and a giggle) 'Thanks, Cadet 52.'

With that, I headed off on my assignment, found the restaurant, picked up the lunches, got back in the car …

Me: 'Cadet 52 to Dispatcher.'

Dispatcher: 'Yes, Cadet 52?'

Me: 'I have the food, and I am on my way back to the station.'

Dispatcher: (another giggle) 'Thanks, Cadet 52.'

I drove to the station and then:

Me: 'Cadet 52 to Dispatcher. I'm 10-7 at the station.'

Dispatcher: 'Cadet 52 (laugh), can you please see your staff sergeant upon your return.'

Me: 'Not a problem, Dispatcher … I have his lunch anyhow for him.'

Dispatcher: (lots of laughter) 'Ok.'

As I walked in the station, my cousin Brian McNeil, who was a detective at the station, laughed at me, shaking his head and walked away. He had just come in from a call. I couldn't understand why he was laughing and didn't say anything to me.

Family And Career

I walked into Staff Sergeant Winter's office and was asked to close the door. Then, I got a harsh talking to about telling the entire division and the dispatchers that I was running to pick up his lunch. Confused, I explained why I had done it, saying that we had been trained to tell them, but he burst out laughing and said that I didn't need to tell them what I was picking up. I certainly didn't live that one down for a long while.

Lesson — Sometimes you don't have to take taught things so literally. We are all taught how to do things, whether that is in school, on the job or by our families. Sometimes it's important to read between the lines and work out the best way to move forward.

I also assisted the detective office or CIB (Criminal Investigation Bureau), as it was known. If there were no female officers around, I would be asked to conduct strip searches on female prisoners who were in custody, especially if they were under arrest for shoplifting or drugs offences. The detectives were not above playing tricks on me either. I certainly had my eyes opened one day when they called me up to search a female prisoner who had been brought in for shoplifting.

She was a beautiful, well-presented woman, wearing very expensive clothing, and as I entered the interview room, I thought, 'Why would she need to shoplift?' Boy, was I naïve! I told her that I was there to conduct a strip search and that she should tell me then and there if she had anything on her she should not have. She stated that she didn't, so I asked her to remove her clothes. Unfortunately, strip searches are a necessary part of policing although not always a nice part. I asked the woman, who was standing in her underwear, to take off her bra, which she did, and then her bottoms. I was immediately shocked as I got an eyeful of her massive penis!

This was new to me, and in a shocked state, I ran out of the room, only to be confronted with all the detectives sitting in a semi-circle, waiting for my quick exit. Flustered, I tried to explain

My Own Learning Begins

myself but was met with laughter from all of them. I had been set up. Even the prisoner, a regular, had been in on it and more than happy to oblige for the new cadet on the block. From that day on, I was always wary about any job the CIB gave me. As a new cadet, I was certainly getting an education on the city of Toronto and its inhabitants. But much of what I learned through my time there, I was able to take with me on my career path.

Lesson — Learn to laugh along at yourself. You will learn that you can love who and what you are, and by laughing at yourself, nothing can hurt you.

From 52 Division, I was then transferred to the Headquarters Duty Desk. They tended to transfer us around a bit to get a look at several different areas. At the Duty Desk, I did a lot of answering phones and transferring calls but also took questions from the public. The other thing I was called upon to do was drive senior officers to meetings if needed. One day, I received a call to get Deputy Cook's car ready as he and Deputy Scott were heading to a meeting just off Yonge Street. It was a winter day, but the weather had started to clear and the roads were starting to resemble slush. Deputy Cook had a big car with a bench seat in it, and as he was about 6'5", I couldn't reach the pedals. I pulled the seat right up, then drove the car to the back door of HQ and waited for them.

As they got in the car, Deputy Cook tried to get in the front seat but couldn't get his legs in properly (as I had pulled the seat forward) so had them at an angle with his knees pointed to the centre of the car. Deputy Scott got in the back. They directed me down Yonge Street and pointed to the street where their meeting was taking place. Not thinking, I made a left-hand turn onto the street, right into oncoming traffic. It was a one-way street, and I was going the wrong way! They both gasped, but without a thought, I pulled up onto the sidewalk, put the car in park and said, 'There you go, sirs!'

Family And Career

Deputy Scott got out of the backseat, giggling. Deputy Cook also tried to get out, but his knees were stuck under the dashboard. I didn't even think to move the seat back, nor did he ask me to. He just put his hands on top of the door frame and tried to pull himself out, which I might add, he did. However, he landed on his butt on the slush-covered footpath. Deputy Scott just started to laugh as Cook pulled himself to his feet, brushing off the slush that was now covering his lovely suit, leaned into the car and said, 'Have a nice day, Cadet Banks.' With that, he closed the door. I was really hoping that they would just walk away, but no, they stood there, waiting to see what I was going to do on this one-way street. There really was nothing I could do except wait for traffic to clear, drive a little bit further to a driveway, turn around and head back to Yonge Street. They waved at me as I drove past them, with Scott still laughing!

No sooner had I got back to my desk than my phone rang. It was my father asking me how my day was going. I knew something was up, and when I said it was okay, he started laughing and said, 'Heard you had an issue driving the Deputies?' Funny enough, I never had to drive them anywhere else from that day onward, and soon after, I was transferred once again, this time to the Summons Bureau.

Lesson — I realised that I would never be able to do anything on this job without my father finding out! It is really important that you do the best you can do because you never know who will be watching and reporting.

When I think back to my job at the Summons Bureau, it is hard to believe that they had unarmed cadets doing this job. We had to deliver summons to people to appear in court in regard to unpaid parking tickets, driving violations and any other summons that may be given to us to serve. Some of the people we served were not of the best quality of citizen. So, it really does boggle my mind that none of us were hurt. The recipient of a summons wouldn't always be the happiest, and on those occasions, we tended to beat a hasty retreat out of their reach. Not sure they would have cadets doing that job in today's society. But all these jobs I had as a cadet certainly gave me an understanding of the world I was about to get into and made me believe even more that I could go out and make a difference!

By the time I was 20 and not far off 21, I was allowed to go into training to become an officer. Our training was done in two parts: first at the Toronto Police training college, C.O. Bick College, where we went each day for training, and then at the Ontario Police College (OPC) in the small town of Aylmer, near London, Ontario, with officers from all other forces around Ontario. We lived in at the OPC and were allowed to go home on weekends. The college enforced strict rules. We were expected to have spotless rooms, perfectly made beds each morning, then parade before classes wearing perfectly polished boots and belts. It was run military-like but for a good reason: they wanted to drill into you the rules and respect for the uniform. It was challenging, but I loved the learning: law, self-defence, firearms, driving skills and how to handle different types of calls and human nature responses.

After graduating from the OPC, we went back to our respective forces for more training on local laws, a bit more self-defence and fitness. At my graduation, I was honoured to be a flag bearer, and my dad, as a senior officer, was there not only as my dad but as part of the senior staff. We were lucky enough to have a picture taken with him saluting as I walked past as part of the flag bearers. It was the only time in my career where my dad had to salute me!

CHAPTER 9
Life In Uniform

'Often, in the real world, it's not the smart that get ahead but the bold.'
~ ROBERT KIYOSAKI

The most exciting part of graduating was finding out where we would be assigned, and I was lucky enough to be assigned to 55 Division in the Beaches area of Toronto. Having grown up in the east end of Toronto, the Beaches weren't too far from home. It was the area my grandmother lived in, where Dad had grown up and where my grandfather had finished his career, so it seemed fitting. I had a great training officer to ride with, James (Jim) Rollo. He had several years on the job, and I learned a fair deal from him. But as a rookie, there are always times when the other officers will play jokes on you. I remember one early evening when we received a call for a jumper off the Bloor Street bridge, meaning someone had jumped to commit suicide. We were told

Family And Career

to go to Bayview Avenue beneath the bridge. When we arrived, numerous emergency services were already in attendance. As we pulled up, our sergeant approached us and told us to just wait for a detail. After a few minutes of Jim speaking with the sergeant, the sergeant approached me and told me that I had to search the roadway for the deceased's teeth.

I was told that, when he had jumped, he had been hit by a car, had lost his teeth and that he had no identification on him. The only way we were going to be able to find out who he was, was through his dental work. I was shocked, but as a brand-new rookie, I had to follow direction from a superior officer. So, as the sun was setting and it was now getting dark, I took my flashlight and started to look at the road to find teeth. I was doing this for about 3-4 minutes, thinking that this was not what I wanted to be doing, when all the officers on the scene started laughing. I had been duped!

I swore to all of them that one day I would get even! To be honest, as the years went by, I did a few things like that, myself, to the rookies that I worked with. It was all just a bit of fun to lighten the mood in times that were so sad. It is such a shock dealing with your first death, no matter how it happens, and it never really gets any better. Laughter is one way to get through it. It may seem harsh to people outside of the emergency services, but without laughter, you would never survive mentally.

I wasn't at 55 Division long before I found out that my father had been promoted and would soon be in charge of the division. To avoid any conflict of interest, I was told that I would be transferred out to the west end of the city to 2 District. This is when I rebelled! I approached my dad and told him it was unfair that I didn't have a choice in the matter. It wasn't my fault that he had been promoted and sent to where I worked, I said, and I shouldn't have to be sent to the other side of the city because of him. For me, this would have meant either moving house or travelling for over an hour to get to work.

He actually agreed with me; I had won my argument. Still, it was with a sad heart that I said goodbye to my first 'police family', and on Monday 14 March 1983, I had my first shift on C Platoon in 54 Division. It was the only time I used my dad to fight my battles for me.

Those divisions were quite distinct in terms of culture and ethnicities. To the south of 54 Division, we had the Greek district on Danforth Avenue, which bordered 55. A lot of public housing spattered throughout the north of the district, industry in the centre, the residential area of East York on the east side and the Don Valley Parkway on the west side. It seemed to be always busy, no matter what time of day it was.

I was one of two women on C Platoon, the other being Lenna Bradburn, who had been on a few years longer than me and who would later go on to become Canada's first female police chief in the city of Guelph, Ontario. Although everyone seemed to welcome me, I didn't feel like I fit in right away. Back then, women were expected to just fit in, be one of the guys. There was no filter for the jokes and language; it was just assumed that if you couldn't handle it, you should get out of the job.

One day after parade, I remember walking down the hallway and overhearing one of the male officers, Jerry Dwyer, saying that I was only on the job because of my father. He was walking behind me, and as I heard this, I abruptly turned, grabbed his shirt front in my right hand and pushed him against the wall. I think everyone in the hallway was shocked, even myself, when I said to him, 'If you have something to say about me, then say it to my face. My dad didn't take the exams to get here or go through the training, I did it myself.' With that, I let go of him, turned and walked out of the building.

Jerry came up to me later and apologised, and we eventually became pretty good friends and colleagues. I don't know if doing what I had done was the right thing, but I felt like I fit in more after

Family And Career

that day because they realised I could stand up for myself. I ended up loving my job in 54 Division and the 'family' that I worked with. We not only worked together but we socialised together. It's funny how policing ends up being your whole life. You deal with unimaginable things that you can't talk to your average friends about because they just wouldn't understand. But you can talk to you work 'family' because they get it!

Lesson — Stick up for and believe in yourself. By being yourself, you can win people over. Too many times, we try to be someone we aren't just to fit in, but in the end are you really happy being someone else? If someone doesn't like you for who you are, then you don't need them in your circle of friends or even acquaintances.

I actually became known as DOA 54 (Dead on Arrival). For some reason, I seemed to get all the calls for the dead bodies. Whether they were suicide, sudden deaths or homicides, if they happened when I was on duty, I always seemed to get the call. Some of them were very traumatic deaths and most just very sad occurrences. If I needed to talk about these types of calls, it would be with my colleagues and not my friends outside of the force. In fact, my first day and my first call at 54 Division was for a suicide. A man had hung himself in his stairwell. I remember it was a very sad case that involved alcohol and a fight with his 21-year-old daughter, who subsequently left the house and came back eight hours later to find her father dead.

I learned so much from the guys and girls at 54 Division and even was awarded Police Officer of the Month in 1984 with one of my work colleagues, Jim Williamson. One day in March 1984, we had been working the 5 pm to 3 am shift, when, at 11 pm, we saw a male come out from the rear area of a Mister Transmission & Midas Muffler shop. Thinking it looked odd at this time of day, I turned the car around and we approached him. We got out of the car, and Jim asked him if he had reason to be in the area, asking if he worked here. He replied that he had been working on a car.

Jim said that it was a bit late to be working and asked him to show him the car. The man was very nervous, looking back at the building and taking his hands in and out of his jacket pockets. As I moved the car, Jim walked to the back of the shop with the man. After parking the car and upon getting out, I heard Jim say, 'Ok, you had better sit in the back seat.'

Before I could put him in the car, I searched him and found three 8-ounce cans of Ronsonol lighter fluid, another 4-ounce can of lighter fluid, a lighter and a flashlight in his front pants pocket. As I put these items on the hood of the car, he became even more nervous. He got to the point when he blurted out, 'You better hurry before it blows!' Well, that's not something you really want to hear. We asked him what he was talking about, and he told us to follow him. He led us to Melodies Restaurant around the corner and pulled vigorously on the front door a few times and the door popped open. We could see smoke in the restaurant, so while Jim and the male entered, I went back to the car, calling for the fire department and assistance.

Jim and the suspect exited the restaurant out the rear door, and the suspect was arrested, placed in handcuffs and into the back of our car. It wasn't long before the North York Fire Department arrived, and they were able to extinguish the fire. After talking to the suspect, we worked out that he had been paid to set fire to the building so the owners could put in an insurance claim. It was a great arrest and one that we kind of fell into, which is how it sometimes happens.

Uniform policing was such a combination of everything. You were sent on calls for everything from minor thefts, domestics, missing people, deaths, neighbour complaints, break and enters, damage to property, dealing with drunks, fights, traffic offences and many other things. But the most important part of the job was being observant, noticing suspicious things and acting on them.

Family And Career

Lesson — If you follow your intuition, you can sometimes make a huge difference.

Intuition is a funny thing because a lot of times we are too fearful to take a leap of faith and follow that intuition. Someone else does and is successful at accomplishing what we could have accomplished. Next time your intuition tells you to have a go, jump in with both feet and trust in it and yourself. You might be amazed at what you accomplish.

CHAPTER 10
Life On The Streets

'Prostitution is a fiercely competitive business.
The rules are simple. The younger the merchandise,
the higher the profits they can draw — but not for themselves.
The money goes to the pimps.'
~ MARY SANCHEZ ('Online sex trafficking flourishing',
San Angelo Standard Times, 17 January 2017)

In 1985, a new law was introduced in Canada in regard to prostitution that stated: 'It is illegal to communicate in a public place for the purposes of engaging the sexual services of a prostitute.' Three elements were necessary to establish that prostitution was taking place: (i) provision of sexual services, (ii) the

Family And Career

indiscriminate nature of the act (soliciting rather than choosing clients), and (iii) the necessity for some form of payment.

The reasons for bringing in this law and, I guess, the concerns voiced by residents in areas where prostitution took place included:

1. The negative effect of prostitutes constantly on the streets.

2. That female pedestrians regardless of age were unable to walk the streets day or night without being approached by passing males in automobiles.

3. The concern that prostitutes attract other criminal elements in the area.

4. That the younger prostitutes are also victims being put to work on the streets by pimps.

5. The rubbish left behind by prostitutes and 'Johns', such as condoms and syringes, which were being found and picked up by local children.

The Toronto Police Force was trying to work out how to enforce this law as there had to be the three elements, as mentioned earlier, in order to prosecute a 'John' (client). I was approached by the Morality Bureau — the unit more commonly known as the Vice Squad — in early 1986 to do a bit of work with them on this law and do some minor undercover work. I would have to stand on a street used by prostitutes, dressed in my normal clothes, and see if cars would stop to ask me for services. If the client asked me for a sex act and offered me a price, I was to alert my backup officers. The officer would then approach the driver, identify himself, and the person would be arrested, then issued with a summons to appear in court.

At 24 years old, I thought this would be exciting! I knew that my mom had done something similar years earlier so felt I really was following in the family footsteps. What I did find out was that standing on a street on a winter's night could be extremely cold. It was interesting though, and the variety of prospective clients

I met was eye-opening. There was every age and profession: tradesmen, businessmen, emergency services workers, lawyers, judges, husbands and grandfathers. Men driving expensive fancy cars, beaten up cars and cars with baby seats in the back. Even though I now had a number of years on the job and thought I had seen it all, a lot of this was surprising to me.

I also learned a lot about sex. Yes, at 24, I was getting a sex education from the street and what the men were asking for. I even got to know a few of the working prostitutes in the area, and they weren't averse to having a chat with us 'fake' girls, telling us about their 'clients' and what they charged for what sex act.

I learned all about the street terms used, such as:

'Trick/John' – a client

'Daddy' – pimp

'Stroll/track' – the area where someone works on the street

'Around the world' – an all-night purchase that took in all sex acts

'Safe sex/sheiks/rubbers/ safeties' – condoms

'Naked' – no condom to be used

'Hand job' – masturbation of a customer

'Turned him' – money has been exchanged and sex act completed

'Bad date' – when a customer harms or rips off a prostitute

'Lay' – vaginal intercourse

'From behind' – anal intercourse

'Blow job' – oral sex/fellatio

'On the game' – working as a prostitute

So as you can see, from a fairly innocent young woman from the suburbs of Toronto, I learned a whole new vocabulary. I also found out about the life of those women of all ages, from young teens (the youngest I met during my time in Morality was 12) to women right up to their late 60s.

We charged a lot of men, but this new law had yet to be tested in court. I remember the first cases that came up in court. The courtroom was packed with media, law students, lawyers, police

Family And Career

officers and the public. There was standing room only. I was sitting in the front row waiting to be called if needed to testify. To say I was nervous is an understatement. I was going to have to stand up in front of this packed courtroom and give evidence if any of the accused persons decided not to plead guilty. The judge this first day was Judge Robert Dnieper.

My first case up this day was a 60-year-old grandfather of Portuguese descent who pled not guilty, so I was called to the witness box. Judge Dnieper would usually sit with his back to the witness box as the evidence was being given, and it was no different on this day. My evidence was that the accused had pulled his car up to me, leaned over, rolled his passenger window down and asked, 'Are you working?' I replied, 'Yes.' He then said, 'I will give you $20 for a blow job.' At this point, Judge Dnieper swung his chair around so fast I thought he was going to fall out of it. 'Officer,' he said, 'can you please tell me what you mean by "blow job"?'

I heard the chuckles and giggles from the body of the court. I was wearing a black-and-blue knit suit with a V-neck, and I could feel the redness rising on my chest to my face. I knew he was doing this to get a laugh and see how I would react. With a look of anticipation on his face, I took a deep breath, looked him straight in the eyes and said, 'Well, your honour, "blow job" is the street term used for the sexual act of fellatio.' His face fell; he swivelled his chair around so that his back was once again to me and under his breath said, 'Thank you.' With that, I was asked to leave the witness box and returned to my seat in the body of the court.

The accused was found guilty and fined. What amount, I cannot remember, but as the man was about to head out of the court, Judge Dnieper stopped him and in a gruff voice said, 'Come back here.' The man was shaking, holding a hat in his hands which he was twisting around nervously as he headed back before the bench. Judge Dnieper, with his elbows on his desk, sitting high above everyone in the room, leaned forward and said, 'Do you know what makes me angry.' In a tiny voice, a quiet 'no' came out of the man standing before him. 'That you only offered this lovely young woman $20. Now get out of my court!' With that, the crowd erupted in laughter, and I just wanted to slide under the bench I was sitting on. I felt that the judge was making a laughingstock of us trying to uphold the new law, but that is what he was like as a judge. The rest of the day went on similarly although Judge Dnieper never did swivel around on his chair to ask me anything on any other case that day.

There were several appeals against this new law, and to be honest, I don't know if it was ever repealed. There were a number of 'sweeps' conducted over the next year, and I think the biggest one was over three days in November 1987 where 442 men were arrested and charged. This law had been in place over a year, but people weren't learning. The lure of a young woman on the street who would do anything asked of them by these men was just too strong. This was my introduction to the next four years of my life working in the Morality Bureau.

Lesson — As long as there are men and women offering to pay for sex, prostitution will never be dead, but we must all work to stop the sex trade of young children and girls. A lot of people believe that this doesn't happen anymore, but believe me, the sex slave trade is alive and well in many big cities around the world. It is so important for all of us to try and stop this from happening.

CHAPTER 11
Prostitution And Pimps

'Evil is powerless if the good are unafraid.'
~ PRESIDENT RONALD REAGAN

It wasn't always about standing on streets waiting to be hit upon. I moved into more 'real' undercover work. Most of my work revolved around the prostitution problem in Toronto, but I also got involved with the Roma (Gypsy) community. Gypsies in Toronto were a huge problem when it came to committing frauds. Many women were 'fortune tellers' with shopfronts fitted out with small rooms to have your fortune told, and some of the men would go door to door selling their roofing or driveway fixing scams.

I was partnered with Constable Terry Wark who had been doing a bit of work with the Roma community. We didn't really work undercover when dealing with them but more so got to know them and investigated them when complaints were made. The local gypsy clan got to know and befriend us — or so they thought.

Family And Career

We even got to understand their language and were invited to one of their weddings. I learned the 'fortune tellers' tricks of the trade, like how to make a hair ball appear from the inside of an egg or tomato, and all about their beliefs.

The Roma culture is fascinating, and the International Romani Union, which represents the Roma people, holds a 'Consultative Status' with the United Nations. I made a number of arrests within the community for the frauds they committed, scamming people out of thousands of dollars. Terry and I ended up giving lectures at the C.O. Bick Training College to officers undertaking the Fraud course to alert them to those scams.

But as I said, most of my work at the beginning revolved around the prostitution problem. Working undercover was fun but could be scary at times. I was being someone I really wasn't but having real identification with a different name, date of birth and address. I learned that it was crucial to know the place you pretended to be from and to use a name and details you would remember. There was a huge problem in Toronto with pimps running young girls, mostly runaways who had come to the big city thinking they were going to find that pot of gold at the end of the rainbow. The problem was that there were people lurking in the shadows to change their direction.

I was asked to pose as one of these young women along with other young police officers. I was teamed up with a policewoman named Deborah Harper. Deb had been working with others in the same capacity for a while before I arrived. Working with two other policewomen, she had been involved in a huge project that had been successful in taking down a whole network of pimps. In fact, Deb and the other two policewomen were named as Police Officers of the Year for their work in this area. So I knew that I would learn a lot from Deb.

Deb and I were sent into a local bar where, according to information we had received, a number of pimps were working.

We posed as girls from out of town, looking to get some work. We were in this bar several nights getting to know the regulars, who in turn asked us all about who we were and why we were there. We had our cover story and stuck to it. We would talk about our day's unsuccessful job hunt and our diminishing funds, explaining that we would soon have to find somewhere else to stay. After about a week, we were considered regulars ourselves and welcomed into the fold.

One man by the name of Tony Provo became very friendly with us, sitting at the table with us every night and asking how the job search was going. As our familiarity increased, he started telling us about how we could make money for ourselves and not have to work for anyone. He said this involved 'dating' men who would pay, making it sound like the easiest job in the world. Each night, he would continue this line of discussion, telling us that, if we had sex with these men, they would pay different amounts for different 'things' (sex acts). We kept telling him we were unsure, and he offered to be our 'bodyguard', in other words, our pimp.

At one point in this developing relationship, he asked to see where we were living. We knew that this would be coming, so we had set up a motel room to look like we had been there for weeks. With clothes strewn around the place, empty takeaway containers on the dressers and our bathroom looking well used, we eventually invited him to come to the hotel. Now, keep in mind that we didn't have backup with us; they were in the peripheral but certainly not like you see in television shows, sitting in a room next door! So we were really on our own back then, having to rely on our own wits.

Seeing our motel room seemed to make Tony relax even more. Eventually, we told him we had found a cheaper room to rent but couldn't have guests because the lady who owned the house had strict rules. This kept us from having to show him where we were supposed to be living.

Family And Career

We also set up a safe phone in our office so that if it rang everyone in the office knew it would be for us so the charade could continue. This seemed to satisfy him. We had somewhere cheap to live and a phone number to be contacted on, so the relationship continued to build. Eventually, near the end of August 1986, he called our safe phone and said he wanted to see us and needed an answer as to whether we wanted to work.

We met him at the Swiss Chalet restaurant on Yonge Street, just north of our office building. He showed up carrying a briefcase, trying to look like a businessman. I was wearing a wire to record our conversation. We needed him to say exactly what we had to do on tape as evidence. The problem back then was that the recording device was the size of an old-style Walkman, so I had put it at the front of my pants with the wire running up to a clip with a microphone on my bra. At the restaurant, we ordered our food, and while waiting for it, the conversation started. He stated that he needed an answer and he needed it tonight. We told him we were really running short on money but didn't know what, how or where we would have to work.

He went on to tell us that we had to dress differently, that we needed some dresses and that, if we were on the streets in what we were wearing now, people would think we were cops. We all had a laugh. If only he had taken his own advice ...

Next, he told us that we needed 'safeties', by which he meant 'condoms', adding that we could get them at the drugstore. He told us that we needed ten each every day that we were 'out there'. When we said that we would be embarrassed getting them, he told us he would buy them for us.

Our conversation was interrupted several times by the waitress coming to take our order and bring our food, so we talked about our lives or, more importantly, Tony's life. We were yet to find out his last name and who he really was, so it was important to try and pull that information out of him. He did tell us that night that he had a child who lived in Montreal and that he wasn't married.

He kept reiterating that we had to only work at night, that it was the best time to work and that we should be charging between $80–$100 for an hour. He explained that if one of us got a date, the other would have to stay in the spot so that we didn't lose it. He also told us not to let any guy push us around and to let him know if we were approached by another guy (pimp). Deb asked what he would do if someone was hassling us, and he replied, 'You don't want to know.'

'We questioned why he was trying to help us and his answer was that even if he didn't know us well he liked us. But he cautioned us not to leave and run back to our town after all his help. He then became quiet.

'You know why I want to help you guys?' he said with a serious look on his face. 'Cause I like you, respect you and I enjoy your company too. But you have to be honest with me. Ya can't lie to me. You lie to me, you kill me. Can I ask you guys a question: are you guys cops?'

'Cops?' I said. 'Why would you think that?'

At that point, we turned it back on him.

'You could be, for all we know,' Deb said.

He was quite surprised, and Deb continued telling him that someone at the Paddock had told us to be careful, that he, Tony, was an undercover cop. Tony was shocked and was adamant that he wasn't a cop, nor did he want to be a cop, nor did he even like cops or want to be around them. This completely changed the focus from us to him and ended that conversation.

Next, he told us where we would work, adding that he would stay around at the beginning to make sure we were okay. After that, we would be on our own. He advised us not to go with a man who was not in a car. If we were taken to a hotel, the date had to pay for it and take us back to where we had been picked up. We were not to charge anything under $80. At this point, we really had everything that we needed to arrest him. Tony was getting agitated thinking that there were undercover police in the restaurant, so he suggested we all go for a walk.

It was time to call our office, but first I had to give Tony an excuse. I told him that we were supposed to go to a party and I had to call our friends to let them know that we weren't coming. I went out to the payphone (no mobile phones back then!) and called our office. I let our Sergeant Phil Wilson know that we had the information needed to prosecute him for Exercise Control and Attempt to Procure. We just didn't have enough for Living off the Avails of Prostitution at this point as he hadn't said that we had to give him the money we made. I told Phil that we would be walking down the street and organised to stop in the coffee shop south of our building, then give him the sign when we walked out of the shop if we were sure we had enough information. I also told him that Tony was carrying a briefcase and I wasn't sure what was in it.

Phil and Constable John 'Fergie' Ferguson were going to be farther down the street waiting for us to come out of the shop. As we were walking to the coffee shop, the conversation continued. We were told that if we got arrested, we were to say nothing about him buying condoms for us. He also asked us if we had ever been with a man and whether it had been an 'older guy or younger guy'. I told him I had been with a 20-year-old man before.

'That's the oldest guy you ever made love to?' he asked.

'Yes,' I said.

Then the conversation changed.

'You have no pimp, right?' he said. 'You have no one that you work for in case you get stopped by the cops. You work cause you need money, you need money for yourself.'

He then proceeded to show us how to walk on the street and how to pace our walk when we are working.

'If you go to jail,' he went on, 'I have a number to give you, alright? But I doubt that you will if you do what I ask you to do. You won't go to jail, alright? Don't get in no fight down there; walk away from a fight. If another girl tries to tell you to get off the street, you know, she don't own the street — you do. She do what she got to do, and do what you got to do. Stick together no matter what. Don't show no fear or look like you are anyway.'

At this point, he stopped us and pointed at two coming out of our office building.

'There's the kinda dates you'll be getting, right there, guys over there,' he said.

It was all I could do not to laugh because it was our sergeant and Fergie!

'Why are you doing this, spending so much time and telling us what's going on,' Deb asked. 'It's just hard to believe that you like us, you know, like you say that if we do what you say and we stand there, it sounds too easy.'

'You could stand out there for hours, ya know, hours, before you can make a dollar, you know,' Tony replied. 'It's not easy. It might look easy, but it's not always that easy. It's how you hold yourself and dress up right. It means you have to look sophisticated all the time.'

Deb asked him if we would have to change the way we look.

'Just a little,' he replied. 'Don't change too much.'

Then he asked, 'So what street you all live on?'

I replied I couldn't remember the name of the street as we had just moved there. When I asked why he wanted the address, he said, 'Could be cops, could be investigators, could be all kinds of things, ok? But I don't feel it. If I felt it, then I wouldn't be helping. I'd stay away from it. I just want to know where, um. I've got the phone where you're at. I have to know where it is.'

I tried to steer away and said, 'I don't even know the number. What is it?'

Deb asked him if he would come to the house.

'No, I would never come there,' he replied.

We were able to change the subject and started chatting about another person from the bar. All of a sudden, Tony said, 'Want to know who I am? Uh? I am Tony, Tony T. I don't know a cop, nor do I want to be one, nor do I want to be around, um, you know … I'm an interior decorator.'

It was then that I asked him if he had pictures of interior decorating in his briefcase.

'Maybe,' he replied. 'Or 5 pounds of coke in there or a pound of hash in there.'

We all laughed, and the conversation continued.

'I wanna help,' Tony said. 'I wanna help you both, but I don't want to be fucked.'

'I don't know why you keep thinking that we're going to do that,' I said. 'It's the third time you've said that.'

'No one helped me, right? I help myself, so I want to help you.'

'So what do you get out of this?' Deb asked.

'What do I get?'

'Ya.'

'Give me what you want to give me, only give me what you want,' he said.

'But how much is that?' Deb asked. 'How much would we make?'

'You could both make $500 a night,' Tony replied. 'So you give me part of that, what you want.'

We then crossed the street as I said I needed to get a cold drink in the coffee shop. While we were crossing, Tony again brought up the fact that he had been told we were cops. He wouldn't tell us who had said this at the bar but said he had made his own judgement and didn't think we were, so he wasn't worried. He then mentioned that we couldn't work tonight as we were dressed appropriately and 'Johns' would think we were cops.

As we approached the coffee shop, I could see that our backup, Sergeant Phil Wilson and Constable John 'Fergie' Ferguson, were just down the street. I went into the shop and bought a drink, and when I came out, Deb and Tony were leaning on the ledge of the front window.

'Tony was just asking what we want to do, right?' Deb told me. 'I'm just saying like that's a lot. Like this sort of thing boggles the mind.'

'Specially the $500. Boggles isn't the word,' I replied.

'Don't expect to get it every time you go out,' Tony said.

'What do you think?' Deb asked.

'Are you going to do it?' Tony asked. 'I've asked you to do it, so do it. Be smart, be brave.'

'We'll be smart and brave,' I replied with a laugh.

At this point, I put my drink down and put both my hands through my hair — my sign to our backup, who were just south of us. It meant that we had the information we needed and they could proceed with the arrest.

Deb, Tony and I continued walking south on Yonge Street while Tony was asking us if we knew self-defence. Phil and Fergie were just ahead of us, and Tony was walking between Deb and me. Phil and Fergie got to the next street, Ramsden Park Road, turned around and started walking back towards us. I could feel Tony's body tense up as we continued to walk, and he stopped talking.

As Phil and Fergie approached us, Phil grabbed Tony by the arms and said, 'Hi, I'm Sergeant Wilson from Morality. You are under arrest.'

Tony started to struggle, and Fergie came from behind him to put his arm around him. Fergie had been eating a peach at the time and it was still in his right hand. When he put his arm around Tony, the peach connected with Tony's nose and face as Fergie said, 'And I'm his friend Fergie.'

Deb and I continued to quickly walk around the corner onto Ramsden Park Road, and I must admit there were a few giggles, thinking about the peach in Tony's nose. As we got around the corner, I was able to switch off the recording device, which was now getting extremely hot against my skin. Tony was transported to the local police station, processed and charged with a number

Family And Career

of prostitution-related charges, such as Attempt to Procure, Exercise Control and Living off the Avails of Prostitution.

By the time Deb and I went back around the corner, Tony was well on his way to the station, so we made our way back to our office to write up our notes and head home for the night. The real work would then begin a couple days later when we had to put the case together for the prosecutor and transcribe the wire. I did find out that it is never a good idea to wear a wire when you are in a restaurant as the microphone picks up everything, including chewing and swallowing!

Lesson — Evil can lurk in the form of seemingly helpful people, so always trust in your gut and instincts. If you don't feel good about a situation, ask for help from others outside of the situation or get out of it. Our gut instinct is there for a reason, and this can help us across many areas of our lives.

Of course, police work isn't all about the excitement and fun of being out on the street working undercover. It was also about paperwork and bringing the accused to justice. Guilty or not guilty, it was up to the court system. But you had to put a good case forward, and it took plenty of time doing the paperwork to make sure your case was airtight. With Tony Provo's case, we had a lot of paperwork to do, including transcribing the tape. This would be entered into evidence during the trial, if there was going to be one.

It took a couple of months. The preliminary trial proved that there was enough evidence, and Tony elected to be tried by a judge and jury. So, a date was set, and Tony's bail was continued until the trial.

That date came, a jury was picked, and we started to produce the evidence. My turn came to be on the stand. This was going to take a while as I started back at the beginning when we first met Tony. I then got to the night of his arrest, questioned about the transcript and what we were told that night. As a lot of the transcript was inaudible, due to the background noise in the restaurant, it was up to me to fill in the blanks. We were lucky that most of the important information was audible.

Tony sat beside his lawyer staring at me with the utmost hatred in his eyes. This always happened in cases like this and especially in Tony's case. He figured that if he asked us if we were cops, we had to tell him, which obviously we didn't have to. Working undercover is all about becoming a very good storyteller, or liar as he would say, in order to have the person you are interacting with believe you. Had Tony gone with his gut feeling, he wouldn't be in this predicament. Moreover, he might have targeted unsuspecting young women who would most likely be working the streets now.

I went through the transcript, focusing on the parts that proved the charges, but Tony's lawyer was fixated on the giggles at the end of the transcript, after the arrest. He wanted to know why we were laughing. I explained the peach incident, which caused some members of the jury to have a giggle themselves; even the judge had a grin. The lawyer asked why I thought that was so funny, to which I replied that if Tony hadn't struggled he wouldn't have ended up with peach up his nose. This stopped this line of questioning. My cross-examination hadn't finished yet when the judge called an end to the day. It would have to continue the next day.

The following morning, we were all ready to go, but Tony was nowhere to be seen. The judge questioned his lawyer about where his client was, but the lawyer had no idea. The judge issued a 'Fail to Appear' bench warrant for his arrest. The jury was called in, thanked and advised that their services would no longer be required. That was the end of Tony's trial. Why he didn't show up, we will never know, but in the months ahead, I moved on to the Drug Squad section of the Morality Bureau and figured that one day Tony would be arrested and would face his time in court again.

About six months later, I was helping the CBC television station with a piece on the drug problems on the streets of

Family And Career

Toronto. I had been asked to go to a café where we knew drug dealing took place so that the CBC could film me for their expose. I again was wearing a wire. This time, the wire could be heard and recorded by a CBC cameraman who was sitting in one of our surveillance vans across the street with one of our sergeants.

I approached the café and spoke with a man out front who I knew to be a dealer. I asked if he had any 'crack' and showed him a $20 bill. He took my twenty, got up from the table and walked into the café. As I watched him go in, I looked into the front window of the café and who was staring back out at me ... Tony Provo. The look of surprise on my face and on his was astounding! He looked at me then at the dealer who was now coming back out. Tony was trying to make his way to the door through the crowd of people. The dealer handed me a small piece of crack wrapped in plastic. I quickly grabbed it, said thanks and left. As I was walking down the street, I asked the CBC man, via the wire, to let our sergeant know there was a wanted man in the café. I described what he was wearing and who he was, and the sergeant was able to let backup officers know which direction Tony had gone after he left the café.

I continued to my partner's car, who at the time was Juri Soorsk, and we headed in the last direction that had been given. Juri decided to take a parallel street and we spotted Tony. I jumped out of the car and gave chase, with Juri still in the car. I was running on the sidewalk, and as I ran onto the road, I fell straight into a pothole and went down with a thud, hearing a loud crack coming from my ankle. As Juri told me later, 'One minute you were there and then you were gone!' So, the glory I thought I would get by not only making the drug buy but also by arresting Tony all these months later was gone in an instant. Juri helped me in the car, and we headed to the local hospital. Tony was arrested by other officers.

Tony Provo never did hear the rest of my evidence. He decided to plead guilty to the charges, instead of continuing the trial. I know that he did some time; however, I don't recall what the sentence was, and I never had any further dealings with him. It was one more 'pimp' off the streets in an ever-growing problem in Toronto.

Lesson — Good things take time. It may take a while, but justice and the outcome you are looking for does prevail. At times, in life, we want things to just happen to the best outcome as fast as possible. You have to have the belief the outcome you want will be possible, but it just might not happen overnight!

CHAPTER 12

Drug Squad Life

'Drugs are a waste of time. They destroy your memory and your self-respect and everything that goes along with your self-esteem.'
~ KURT COBAIN

I then moved over to the Drug Squad permanently. I had a successful career in the prostitution area, putting away a number of high-profile pimps and getting a few girls off the street. But the girls were so entrenched in the lifestyle, I'm not sure how many stayed off the street or cleaned themselves up from the drugs they had become addicted to. For me though, it was time to move on, and that came in the form of the drug section of the Morality Bureau.

Each district of Toronto had its own Drug Squad. We were there to assist those squads in any way possible, but we also did a lot of work with the federal police and border security. My introduction to the Drug Squad was purchasing illicit drugs in the Ontario housing projects where street-levels drugs were rampant. Buying from the street, we were hoping to move up to find the suppliers. Once we knew the street level dealers, we would ask for larger amounts so that they would introduce us to the next person in the chain.

The housing projects were like rabbit warrens, with numerous corridors and elevators that got you turned around unless you knew the building. I would be sent into these buildings to try and buy drugs but was told NEVER to leave the front door area. That way, backup who were hiding locally could still see me. I would never go in with any identification or wearing a wire. Too many times, you would get a pat down or your pockets searched if they didn't know you.

I remember the one and only time I disregarded what I had been told. Instead of staying at the front door, I was told to follow this guy to the dealer. He took me up the elevator then through hallways, turning corners and up some stairs, at which point he told me to wait in the stairwell, taking my money with him. I figured I had just lost my money, and, in my head, I was berating myself for having followed him. Here I was, stuck in a stairwell, being told to wait, and I really had no idea how I would get out in a hurry if I needed to. And to make it worse, the stairwell was filthy and stank of urine. It was so bad, I was trying to breathe through my mouth and not my nose.

At that moment, five big black men came through the door on the next floor up, including the one who had taken my money, came down the stairs and surrounded me. One of them, who had the longest dreadlocks I have ever seen, spoke to me in a thick Jamaican accent.

'So you want a twenty rock?' He asked, referring to the $20 of crack I had asked for.

'Ya, that's what I told your man,' I said, making myself sound put off. 'I don't know what the fuck the problem is. He took my twenty, and I just want it so I can go back to my man and get high.'

I could feel my legs shaking under my jeans. I just wanted to get the hell out of there. My backup had no idea where I was, and I knew that I was going to cop a huge spray for leaving the foyer of the building.

'My man never seen you before, so I just wanna check you out,' the man with the dreads said. It was obvious that he was in charge.

'Shit, man, if you don't have any, just give me my money back and I'll go find it somewhere else,' I said, trying to sound angrier. 'I'm visiting with my old man and my friend Angie said you guys were good. She lives over in building 10, but happy to do business with someone else.'

Even though I had made up 'Angie in building 10', he nodded his head and my explanation seemed to suffice. He put his hand in his front pants pocket and pulled out a little plastic wrap with a rock in it.

'Here,' he said. 'Just making sure ... You like it, you come back.'

With that, I grabbed the plastic, turned and walked to the stairwell door. But before I left, and even though I wanted to get the hell out of there, I turned to him.

'By the way, nice dreads,' I said. 'How long is your hair without the dreads?'

He looked at me with a sly smile and said, 'Same length baby, same length.'

After that, I walked through the stairwell door and tried to remember how I had been brought through the building. The first elevator I saw, I took, and looked at the emergency map to see how to get out. I went down one floor, then out of the elevator, around the corner and on to another elevator to the lobby just in case they were following me. I couldn't get out of that building quick enough; my heart was beating so fast, it felt like it was going to fly out of my chest. When I got through the front door, I sucked in fresh air, trying to get rid of the urine smell that seemed to have permeated all through me and continued to the spot where I was to meet my backup.

Family And Career

Boy, did I cop it when I got there. It was the only time I disregarded what I had been told to do for my own protection. I was very lucky that night that I could think on my feet and didn't find myself in a whole lot of trouble. In fact, my backup told me that they were only minutes from storming the building to find me! That would have undone a lot of previous work done by others to learn who the dealers were. Never again did I disregard what I had been told to do, especially for just $20 of crack!

Working on this project, I also learned that the dealers were a sad lot of people and pretty stupid. There was one young guy I bought from on three different occasions over a number of months. Each time I made a purchase, he was arrested and charged.

On the third time to court, after giving my evidence, the judge looked at me and asked, 'Are you telling me that you have bought drugs from the accused three times and you've been involved in arresting him three times?'

When I told him yes, he looked at the accused, shaking his head.

Once all the evidence had been produced, the judge told the accused to stand up.

'You must be stupid to sell to the same person so many times and be arrested by her!' he told the accused. 'I see that the last two times you haven't done any jail time ... well, this time, that will change.'

He then sentenced him to six months jail. This was pretty big because almost all or our arrests from this project usually ended up with fines, unless their record was atrocious.

Lesson — Never disregard what you are taught by others who have been there before. No matter what you do in life, there will always be others who have been through the same thing. It's important to find those people and learn from them so that you can avoid making the same mistakes. Mentors are a great thing as they will save you a hell of a lot of heartache and possible failure.

I was lucky enough to work with some incredible officers in my time in the Drug Squad, and one of those was Sergeant Ron

McCracken. Ron was a big man with bushy hair and a full beard and could have passed for a very mean biker! But he really had a heart of gold. In the early part of February 1988, Ron and I were posing as a couple and started hanging out at the Canada House Tavern at Sherbourne Street and Queen Street East. There had been a number of complaints about people trafficking drugs in the tavern.

We went in each night and got to know the locals. Our story was that we were from out of town and Ron was looking for work in the area. We spent enough time in there that the locals took us into their confidence. Eventually, we were invited to the 'main' table, where the dealers sat. We got to know three locals who were all dealing something different. We started hanging out each night with Richard who was dealing hash and hash oil, and Danny and Nick who were dealing in LSD, hash and marijuana.

Sitting here at this tavern just shooting the breeze with these men, I learned that even though they were bad guys, they all had the same life problems that we had. Nick was a father and grandfather, and although he was associated with a biker gang and had done time for attempted murder, he had the same issues with his kids and grandchildren as anyone else. Over the month that I spent with him, each night I came to know all about his family and the issues they had. At times, I even forgot that he had a very mean and scary streak running through him.

Ron had been buying from all of them over the month, and it came to the point where we were now locals and expected in the tavern each night. This can be tough on you because not only are you working each night until after midnight, but you have to go to court during the day if you have any other trials happening. And it just so happened that one day I was spotted by one of the tavern locals outside one of the courts. There was a surprised look on her face when she spotted me, and I quickly got out of the area. I was able to make my way to our court office and asked them to update the court list outside of the court. I had them add my undercover name to the bottom of the list. I knew that she would be making a beeline to someone at the tavern to let them know that I may not be who I was saying I was.

I let the team know what had happened, and we decided upon a story to tell that night at the tavern. We weren't getting the quantity that we were hoping for in this project anyway, so Ron would tell them that we were heading back home as he couldn't find work. I, on the other hand, would take Nick aside and tell him a tale.

That night, as we walked into the tavern, I could feel the eyes on us. Ron walked over to the bar to order drinks and have a chat to the bartender. I headed straight over to Nick and pulled him aside, saying that I needed to speak to him urgently. He guided me to another table, and we sat down.

'Nick, I need you to do something for me,' I said.

'You do, do you?' Nick replied, sounding very suspicious of me.

'Yes. You see, two weeks ago, I was charged with possession of hash. It was the chunk of hash that Ron bought from you, remember? Well, some cop caught me in the donut shop up on Jarvis, and I was issued a ticket to go to court today. I didn't tell Ron because I thought I could deal with it myself. I knew that he would be really mad, and I didn't want to cop a beating from him. Well, I went to court today and they wouldn't finish up the case. They want me to come back in two weeks, and now Ron wants to go home next week. I really, really need you to tell him for me … please,' I said, pleading with him.

'Shit, Carol, I can't believe you haven't told him,' Nick replied. 'Sherrie told me that she saw you in court today and wondered why you were there.'

'Nick, you have to tell him for me. I'm scared shitless of what he will do,' I pleaded with him, almost to the point of crying.

'Ok, I'll tell him. I'll make him see it's not that bad,' Nick replied.

I could see that Ron was making his way over to our table with our drinks, and as he sat down with a grin on his face, he shook hands with Nick. I had moved over a chair so that Ron could sit between Nick and me. Nick turned to Ron.

'Now Ron,' he said, 'I want to have a chat with you about something.'

'Ya, what's up?' replied Ron.

'So, there is something that Carol hasn't told you, and she's a bit worried about telling you because of how you will react.'

Ron turned to me with a scowl on his face, then turned back to Nick.

'So what is it?' Ron asked.

'Well, a couple of weeks ago, Carol got charged with possession of hash,' said Nick.

All of a sudden, Ron flew out of his chair, pushing the table, spilling all of our drinks, and yelling at me, 'You stupid bitch!'

This is not what I was expecting and it scared the hell out of me. I jumped out of my chair because he looked like he was going to hit me. Nick jumped up and grabbed Ron.

'Stop, man,' he yelled. 'It's not that bad.' He pulled Ron back towards him, leaned down and picked up Ron's chair saying, 'Sit down, man, sit down.'

The whole tavern had stopped, everyone looking our way, as Nick guided Ron to sit and I tried to pick up the spilled drinks and pull the table back to where it should have been.

Ron kept his eyes on me, with a look of hatred. If I hadn't known him, I would have thought he would have killed me right then.

'Stupid bitch. What have you done, stupid bitch,' he kept saying under his breath.

'Look man, it's not that bad,' Nick said, trying to calm him down. 'She has no record; she'll just get a fine. Don't worry about it.'

'Ya, but I wanted to go home next week, now we can't,' Ron replied. 'Hell, maybe I'll just leave you here,' he said, directing his comment to me.

'I'm so sorry, babe. I'm so sorry,' I said, trying to grab his hand and play my part. 'I thought I could deal with it today. I know I should have told you, but I was scared to. I'm so sorry.'

Family And Career

Nick kept talking to Ron to try and calm him, while I went to the bar and ordered a couple more beers and grabbed a cloth to wipe up the mess on the table. By the time I got the table wiped, had gone back for the drinks and came back to the table, Nick had Ron laughing about something and it seemed like all had been forgotten. The tavern crowd was back to normal after Ron's outburst, and my excuse as to why I had been in court had worked. Nick even gave me a piece of hash that night to replace the one I had lost when I had been charged. So I figured that my cover had worked!

When we left the tavern that night, I told Ron that he had scared the hell out of me and that we hadn't agreed that he was going to react like that. He said that the less I knew ahead of time, the better, so that I really looked scared of him. Well, he certainly accomplished that! We had a good laugh about it as we headed back to the office to hand the hash to the exhibits officer. But we knew it was time to take the project down and make the necessary arrests. That had been too close a call, and we weren't getting the amounts of drugs or the contacts up the chain that we hoped for. These guys were all really low-level players, and they weren't about to introduce us to anyone bigger up the chain.

We decided that we would make the arrests on 4 March. We were going to invite everyone to a going away party. Not knowing if anyone at the tavern would have weapons, we organised to have the Emergency Task Force (ETF) and 51 Division Major Crime Unit (51MCU) attend to help us make the arrests. I was wearing a wire to let them know when to come in to secure the area while the arrests were being made. Ron and I got to the tavern at 8.35 pm, walked in and sat with the people we knew. None of our targets were there yet.

Nick and Danny came in and sat with us, but one target, Richard, who Ron had been making purchases from wasn't there. Ron questioned everyone as to where Richard was and found out he was at home. Ron excused himself, saying that he had to go and see Richard and left me at the tavern with Nick and Danny. Ron was able to go to Richard's house and arrest him, then come back to the tavern. Once he was back, he made it look like he was giving me a kiss and whispered that they had Richard and to let the team outside know that we were ready for them to come in and secure the building.

Nick and Danny had gone out the side door into a little alleyway to have a smoke of marijuana, which we knew was okay because there was nowhere for them to go. So I made my way into the bathroom to let the team know to come in, via the wire. As there were other women in the bathroom, I went into one of the stalls and started singing, 'It's a go, it's a go, it's a go, go, go.'

'Wow, you must be smoking some good stuff,' one of the women said to me.

'Ya, man, it's great!' I replied.

I exited the stall, pushing myself between them to wash my hands and still singing, 'Go, go, go.' When I left the bathroom, the women were laughing with me.

As I walked out of the bathroom and towards the table, every door into the tavern was pushed open and ETF members wearing all black and carrying large guns came through, yelling for everyone to stay where they were. Everyone froze; the band went silent. Then, one of the 51 MCU sergeants jumped on the stage and, using the band microphone, told everyone just to stay where they were.

Nick, Danny and a female were still out in the little alleyway having their smoke so knew nothing of what was going on inside. I looked at Ron and said, 'Please, let me do it.' I walked to the door, knocked on it, and Danny, who was taking a drag on a spliff, opened it. I had my badge in my hand and said, 'I think you guys should come in here.' He dropped the spliff on the ground, stomping it out, and with a shocked look on his face, he led the others through the door into the tavern.

Family And Career

I advised Nick and Danny that they were under arrest for trafficking, read them their rights and they were handcuffed and taken to the station by members of 51MCU. I will never forget the surprise on their faces or on the faces of all the people in the tavern we had gotten to know over the last month. Funny enough, as we left the tavern, the band started playing again, the crowd noise started up and it was like we had never been there. There is no doubt in my mind that, although we removed the three dealers from the tavern, someone would be back in there, maybe not the next day or week but eventually, taking the spots of Richard, Nick and Danny.

At the time, I was dating a policeman by the name of Don who worked in 5 District Traffic. Ron and I headed over to 51 Division to start processing the arrests. When we got to the station, we took the three accused out of the cells and upstairs to the CIB office to process them. We put Richard and Danny in separate interview rooms and had Nick sitting, handcuffed to a bench in the office. While doing the paperwork, Ron and I did our usual banter, back and forth across the desks, with Nick looking on in bewilderment.

My boyfriend, Don, happened to have a person in the station under arrest as well, and hearing that I was there, he made his way up to see me. We chatted for a few moments, finding out when each one of us would be off work and where we would meet after work.

Once this conversation was over and Don left the office, Nick, still handcuffed to the bench, looked at me and said, 'Carol, what are you doing? What about Ron?' He couldn't comprehend that Ron and I were partners at work, and not life partners as we had been pretending to be. I explained this to Nick, who sat there shaking his head, trying to wrap his thoughts around this.

'Geez, you guys are good,' he said, looking up at Ron and I. 'You sucked me right in. I was sure that you were a couple. You are so good that how can I plead not guilty. You got me dead to rights.'

It is always interesting to deal with old-time crooks who have been around the block more than once. Nick had been through the court and jail system several times, and he knew when he had been caught red-handed. So at the first chance he got, he pled guilty to all the charges against him, whereas Danny didn't, went to trial and was subsequently found guilty anyway. All three we had arrested spent time in jail, and I always wonder whatever happened to Nick, even all these years later.

Lesson — Crime is infectious. When one bad element is removed, others then replace it. No matter how hard we would work, there would always be someone to fill in for the ones we had arrested. It was keeping us in business, and we knew we would never be out of work no matter how hard we fought.

> *'The infectiousness of crime is like that of the plague.'*
> ~ NAPOLEAN BONAPARTE

CHAPTER 13

Criminal Investigations

'Follow the clues of investigation to breakthrough.'
~ STEVEN MAGEE

Four years of the Morality Bureau was enough for me, and I decided that it was time for a change. I applied and was accepted to move into the Criminal Investigation Branch (CIB) at 14 Division. This station was located in the west of the city centre, in an area known as Parkdale. Parkdale had once been an affluent area of Toronto with large Victorian terrace holiday homes. It was now mostly working-class people, migrants and refugees who lived in low-rise apartments and public housing.

It was a mix of cultures with Chinatown on the east side, little Portugal on the north, and, to the west and south of Parkdale, a great mix of Caribbean, Indian, Vietnamese, Filipino, Tamil, Tibetan, Hungarian and Roma people. In the south, many old homes had been turned into accommodation for patients released

Family And Career

from nearby psychiatric hospitals to integrate them into the community. So 14 Division was an extremely busy station dealing with every conceivable crime you could imagine. I thought this would be one of the best places to learn how to be an investigator.

There, I was very lucky to work with some amazing people who taught me how to be meticulous and thorough while investigating a crime. I was first paired with Detective John Boyce, and then for most of my time in the office, I was partnered with Detective Kim Carr. Kim was a superb investigator who went on to become a homicide detective and was also classified as an expert fire investigator. To be able to work with these men was an honour.

One case, however, really made me look at my life and career. It became a defining moment in my career, casting doubts on whether I should stay on the job.

Over a number of years in the late 1980s, there were a series of rapes and sexual assaults in an area known as The Annex. This was an area of lovely Victorian homes, some of which had been converted into apartments. The attacks would start and stop, some coming in clusters. It was believed to be the work of one man who was dubbed 'The Annex Rapist'.

In May 1990, a young woman was coming home late at night from working as a waitress. She had finished work and stayed behind to have a drink with some co-workers. She rented the bottom floor of one of these homes, and the entrance to her apartment was through a side gate into the backyard, where her door was located.

She had made it into her secure backyard and had to go to the toilet so bad that she decided to just squat, have a pee and then get into the house. While in the process of doing this, a man jumped over the backyard fence. She screamed when she saw him, but he continued towards her and told her to be quiet, saying that he wasn't going to hurt her. As he grabbed her by the arms, he kept telling her to calm down and walked her over to her door. Forcing her to open her door, he then pushed her into her flat.

Once she had opened the door, she noticed that he appeared very high and paranoid. As he made her sit on the end of the bed, he told her that he had some cocaine and wanted her to do some of it with him. She was so scared that she accepted, hoping that this would stop him from hurting her, that once she had done this, he would leave.

After doing the line of cocaine, he pushed her back onto her bed. She attempted to kick and knee him in the groin, but he put his hands around her throat, pushing his thumbs into the front area of her neck, cutting off her airway. Fearing for her life, she stopped fighting, thinking that if she just let him do what he wanted, he would leave. He then pulled her pants off, put on a condom and tried to have intercourse with her but failed. He then performed oral sex on her, rolled her on to her stomach and performed intercourse on her. As she started to cry, the man rolled off her and seemed to become remorseful saying, 'What have I done? I have never done that before.'

The man then grabbed a towel, wiped himself off, asked the victim for money and then fled the scene. The victim was so distraught that she just locked the door and lay on her bed crying, too scared to call the police because she felt that she was at fault for letting him in. Unfortunately, believing they are at fault is all too common for women.

Two weeks later, as the victim was asleep in her bed, she was awoken by the sound of someone breaking down her front door. Before she could get to the phone to call the police, there was a man inside her room and beside her bed. She recognised him as the same man from two weeks earlier. Fearing for her life, she didn't scream, and the man not only raped her, again using a condom, but tried to force her to perform acts on him, and when she refused, he started choking her. He repeatedly assaulted her over the course of five hours. After he left her apartment, she phoned the police to report the crime.

Family And Career

After the assault, the woman underwent an examination at hospital and gave her statement to Detective David Needham, the investigating officer in this case. She was then driven home by uniform officers from 14 Division. While stopped at a traffic light, she pointed to a man in the crowd on the sidewalk and said, 'That's him.' The officers radioed for backup and the man was arrested. This was the best identification that an investigator could want as the suspect was in amongst numerous other people.

The man was then taken to 14 Division to be investigated and charged. After being interviewed, he was charged with two counts of choking, two counts of sexual assault and one count of Obstruct Police as he had lied about his name when arrested. Those charges took into account the first assault at the beginning of May, which the victim had finally told the investigators about, and the one earlier that day.

Because of the similarities to the other rapes in The Annex area, I was asked to work with Det. Needham, to investigate whether this man could be The Annex Rapist. The man's name was Richard Gagnon, and the more I looked into his background, the more I learned how evil he was.

He had spent most of his life behind bars, starting from the age of 14. When arrested for this crime, he had already been recommitted to jail five times in the past ten years for parole violations, had three counts of escaping custody and two counts of armed robbery. He was also presently out on bail for possession of cocaine. He had been in jail so many times that he actually obtained his grade 12 high school education while in jail. Needless to say, he was not a very nice man.

I had to pull out the other cases of The Annex Rapist and go through the victims' statements. I looked at the dates of the assaults, comparing them to Richard Gagnon's time out of jail. Almost all of the dates coincided. It was also interesting to compare the way the rapes had occurred, and in all cases, there was no DNA found as the accused had used a condom. But what all the victims did say was that the accused had an unusual smell to him. Unfortunately, none had seen the perpetrator's face, so we had no one that could identify their attacker. This was the one difference to the present case.

Gagnon had spent a lot of his jail time at the Kingston Penitentiary in Kingston, Ontario, which is about 260 km from Toronto. So Det. Needham and I decided to head there to speak with guards and inmates about Richard Gagnon. Everyone we spoke to described him as a sexual predator. It didn't matter whether you were male or female, anyone was prey. When his name was mentioned, some of the inmates even had a look of fear on their faces. When even hardened criminals are scared of a man, you know you're dealing with evil. He was a remorseless criminal who, when he was charged or stood before the courts, took things very lightly and thought it was a joke.

This investigation took time, and despite all our work, we were unable to actually link Gagnon to The Annex rapes. But we still had him on our charges, and he had decided to plead not guilty and opted for a trial by judge alone.

This was very hard on the victim. She had to get in the witness box and describe everything he had done to her, in detail, in open court and have a lawyer try to discredit her. It was very embarrassing and hard for her to do. Her private life was thrown open to the world. She, like most other sexual assault victims, was questioned about all details of her life:

• Did she have any alcoholic drinks after work and before coming home on that first night in question?
• Did she ever do illicit drugs before, and was she a regular user?
• What was her sexual history?
• What was she wearing?
• Why did she decide to pee in her own backyard?

This is one problem with the judicial system in that the accused is presumed innocent until proven guilty, but the victim has to account for everything she does. To be honest, what do these questions matter? She was forced into her own home and assaulted. It had nothing to do with whether or not she was inebriated, what she was wearing or whether she had ever done drugs or had sex before.

It is no wonder women don't report sexual assaults more often when lawyers ask such questions in open court. It is as though the victim is in the wrong for everything she does. Even after all these years, I don't believe that we have moved very far from this.

The one sticking point and one that the defence lawyer was picking on was that she had agreed to do some cocaine with Gagnon minutes before the first assault. He was trying to get the court to believe that she wanted to have sex with him because she was happy to do cocaine with him. He wanted to prove that she did this not out of concern for her own safety, but because she wanted to.

The trial went on for several days, and once all evidence was produced and defended, the judge adjourned to examine the evidence and return his verdict. The trial had been very hard on the victim, and she decided that she wouldn't return to hear the verdict. It would be what it was, and she felt she had to move on with her life.

All these years later, I can't remember exactly how long it took for the judge to return with his verdict, but I will never forget what he said, and I am really happy that our victim wasn't in court.

The judge waffled on for a bit, then said, 'On the first count of Sexual Assault, Miss Jane Doe (I have changed her name) was obviously happy to do drugs with Mr Gagnon and therefore invited him into her home. I believe that Miss Doe had sex with Mr Gagnon and then was remorseful about it and decided that she needed to cry rape. I therefore find Mr Gagnon not guilty. As for the second count, the victim brought this on herself by having sex with him the first time, and at no time, did she tell him to stop or fight back, so I find Mr Gagnon not guilty. I am, however, finding him guilty of damaging property, namely Miss Doe's front door.'

I was incensed, as were the rest of the investigative team. Although Gagnon was back in jail due to a breach of his parole, this meant that he would be out once again, free to commit more crimes. Our victim was so scared of this man that she quit her job and moved house so that he wouldn't know where she worked or lived. Her workplace had come out in court.

I was certainly happy that I wasn't the one who had to tell her the verdict, and I know that once she heard, she was devastated. All I could think of was that if the victim had been the judge's daughter or wife, he would have thought differently!

After all the work we had put into this case, I started to wonder whether I wanted to continue on the police force. It felt like we were banging our heads against a brick wall. I was exhausted of constantly having judges think the way that this judge did. I decided I needed to take some time off.

I applied for a year-long leave of absence to really get away from the job and see if I missed it at all. I was lucky that I was granted the leave, and in November of 1992, I headed to Australia to spend my year travelling and thinking about what I wanted out of life.

Lesson — Live your own life. You can make great money in a job that you dislike, or you can take a pay cut and do something that truly makes you happy.

Sometimes, in life, we do what may be expected of us by others and we stay in jobs or situations that we aren't happy in. It is important to live your life to the fullest and to do something that you truly love. Life is too short to be unhappy, no matter what is causing that unhappiness.

As Hugh Hefner said: 'Life is too short to be living somebody else's dream.'

CHAPTER 14
Travel Adventures

'Jobs fill your pockets, adventures fill your soul.'
~ AWAKENMINDSET.COM

In 1992, with growing uncertainties over my professional future, I decided to take a leave of absence from the force and head to Australia. I had always been fascinated by the country and had been travelling there as often as I could. Unfortunately, I could only go during my holidays, and this was usually only two to three weeks at a time — certainly not enough time to see the country like I wanted to. So with approval from my bosses for the leave, I booked a ticket to Melbourne to start my journey there.

At least, I wasn't going in unaware thanks to my previous trips 'down under'. I was making my home base with a couple who were like second parents to me, Margo and John Howe. Luckily for me, John had a 1976 Ford Falcon car with dual fuel, petrol and LPG, which he kindly leant to me to head off on my travels. It was

Family And Career

late-November and the summer months were just starting, so a perfect time to start this year-long adventure.

After arriving and giving myself time to adjust to the jet lag and time difference, I decided that I would take the next couple of months to explore the state of Victoria. I was on no time clock so could do what I wanted. This also gave me time to organise what I would need to take with me on my journey by car.

As the New Year came and went and I had seen most of Victoria, it was time to say goodbye to John and Margo and begin my road trip. I decided, with a bit of help and some inspiration from the Herald Sun travel section, that I would head to Corryong in the High Country of Victoria as my first destination. The High Country Festival was about to start, with things like gumboot throwing, whip cracking, boiling billy, mountain horse racing and with an Australian Country Bush dance to take place. So in March 1993, with a two-man tent, my little gas stove and a bicycle on the back of the car off, I headed on the journey of a lifetime.

Corryong is a magical small town high up in the mountains, a typical country town with one pub on the main street. Its claim to fame is Jack Riley, the original 'Man from Snowy River', who is buried in the cemetery there. With one caravan park on the outskirts of town, I made my way there, paid for a site, set my tent up and headed back into town to the pub — the best place to find out about a town, its people and events that weekend, and what a weekend it turned out to be. I met some incredible people and saw some amazing horse racing down the side of the mountain. It was fascinating to watch men and women on horseback around a circuit, whip cracking tiny pieces of paper on popsicle sticks! Imagine going as fast as you can on a galloping horse around a circuit, and every 20 metres, you have to break a tiny piece of paper close to the ground with your whip. The winner was the fastest horseperson and the one who had broken the most pieces of paper! To say I was impressed is an understatement.

This was the perfect start to an amazing journey. It was then time to start making my way north. My ultimate goal was to reach Port Douglas, Queensland, to visit a friend I had living there. Over the next three weeks, I would stay and camp at some of the most beautiful spots, including:

- Tumut — hiking the Hume & Hovell Walking Track along the beautiful Goobragandra River and with my heart beating fast cross a wire swing bridge called 'Jack Cribbs Bridge' as it moved below my feet in the wind and rain. Oberon — a small town on the west side of the Blue Mountains where I was able to visit the Jenolan Caves, then head to the Kanangra-Boyd National Park. This area has magnificent scenery with sheer sandstone walls and beautiful trails that lead you down to view some of the parks waterfalls. Very much alone here I felt like I could yell at the top of my voice and no one would hear me.
- Katoomba — a perfect spot to view the 'Three Sisters', an unusual rock formation in the Blue Mountains. Then on to Katoomba Falls with water running down 244m of rock and rides on the Skyway, Cableway and Railway
- Port Macquarie — a stunning coast line, with a caravan park so close to the cliffs I could hear the waves crash on to the beach at night
- Byron Bay — a transient type of town, people of all genders and ages enjoying the most exquisite beach with beautiful sunrises and sunsets.
- Surfers Paradise — a real surfer's paradise as the name suggests
- Noosa Heads — a very picturesque little town wih beautiful homes that sit on a waterway throughout.
- Keppel Sands — almost just a little blip on the map but the soil becomes very red here and almost like being halfway between tropical and bushland. Also a place where you can learn firsthand about cane toads.
- Airlie Beach — gateway to the Whitsunday Islands with beautiful snorkeling and scuba-diving.

- Townsville — a fairly small city but the largest in northern Queensland and reminded me a lot of Perth. It was the first real area that I noticed a lot of indigenous residents, the first area that this really stood out to me.
- Magnetic Island — a lovely boat ride from Townsville the island is bike friendly, although a bit hilly and lovely beaches. A beautiful place to just relax.

During my three weeks of travel up the coast it was incredible the number of people I met not only from Australia but from around the world, doing exactly what I was doing. I enjoyed some fantastic conversation and there was not one person that I didn't like. At times I wanted to spend more time with them but my journey was calling me. I finally reached Port Douglas at the beginning of April 1993, some 3,500 km later.

It had been a while since I had seen my friend Lyn, but we picked up right where we had left off. She was a Melbourne girl who had relocated with her husband, Gerard, to this beautiful part of the world near the Daintree Rain Forest at the top end of Australia. Lyn introduced me to some amazing people who in turn introduced me to another way of life completely. I learned how to scuba-dive on the Great Barrier Reef, even going on to get my advanced diving certificate. I sailed on some magnificent boats, swam in beautiful freshwater ponds and rivers in the forest and really saw how some of the wealthy people of our world live.

My visa for Australia came with one condition: it was valid for a year but I could only stay for six months at a time. So when my six months were coming near, I had to work out where to go, outside of Australia, before I could come back. As I was at the top end, I looked to Papua New Guinea. The travel agent in Cairns was able to get me on a three-day tour, flying into Port Moresby and then on to Mount Hagen, where I would tour the local area. This was perfect because I could then come back to Australia and continue my trip from Port Douglas. This also meant I had somewhere to leave all my belongings while I went.

Travel Adventures

Papua New Guinea

When 17 May arrived, Lyn dropped me off at Cairns airport. As I was checking in, the airport staff told me that they could get me on a flight directly to Mount Hagen, saving a couple of hours. Perfect, I thought. As the plane touched down in a very wild and remote place, I could see the local children on the other side of the wire fence surrounding the airstrip. Barefoot, in shorts and ripped T-shirts, they were standing on the dry, dusty dirt with their fingers gripping the fence, their faces pressed hard up against it, to look at this big bird that had just landed out of the sky.

As I walked down the stairs from the plane door, the heat from the sun and the tarmac was incredible, and I realised that this was going to be a very warm three-day tour. Waiting in line to go through immigration and customs, I could see the others from my flight, all Australian miners heading back to work, had a pink piece of paper with their passports.

When I asked the man in front of me what the paper was, he told me that it was the visa needed to get into the country. This was when I realised there was a reason I was supposed to go to Port Moresby first, and panic set in. The man in front of me was fantastic. He told me to put 10 kina (the local currency) on top of my passport when I handed it to the officer and he would just let me into the country.

I couldn't believe I was about to bribe an immigration officer. The nerves set in, and I was really worried about what would happen. The man in front of me could see the concern etched on my face but told me not to worry, that it would be fine, just not to make a big deal of it. As I stood there, moving closer to the immigration officer with each passport he stamped, I could feel the sweat trickling down my back, my heart beating faster and my hands starting to tremble. All I could think of was those movies where people get arrested in a foreign third-world country and thrown into a hellhole of a jail.

With three people in front of me before I reached the counter, I was looking around, but there was nowhere to go and nothing I could do to change the situation. I just had to do what the man in front of me had said and quietly bribe the officer.

Sure enough, when I got to the counter and was asked for my passport, I had the 10 kina ready and said that I didn't have a visa, trying to explain what had happened in Cairns with the airline changing my flight. The officer grabbed my passport and the money, quickly pocketing the note, waved his hand, and with no questions asked, he stamped my passport and let me walk through. It was like he didn't even want an explanation, just the money.

As I walked past fully armed officers, my legs were shaking and my heart was feeling as if it was going to force its way out of my chest. I figured, as long as no one else saw my bribe and I could get out of immigration, I would be fine. I walked past the counter and out to collect my bag, and the relief that washed over me was staggering.

That was my first criminal offence, and it had happened in a developing country!

As I waited for my luggage, my heart started to return to normal, but looking around, I certainly felt out of place: a single white blond-haired female amongst dark-skinned people. I felt like I was a beacon with a sign over my head saying, 'Look at me, look at me. I'm different!' I now know how others feel when they immigrate to countries completely different to theirs and they are the minority.

The airport was extremely basic, with the luggage brought out by hand and handed to you. Once I retrieved my suitcase, I had to find the tour guide. I was two hours early so thought I may have to wait. But to my surprise, I found a vehicle outside the terminal with the name 'Plumes and Arrows Resort' on the side of the door. A man was leaning against it, smoking. I approached him and asked if he was waiting for a Carol Banks. He looked at a piece of paper in his hand and said no, he was waiting for Mr Carl Banks. I told him that it was in fact me, that I wasn't a Mr but a Miss, and not Carl but Carol. This took him completely by surprise, and the stunned look on his face was an interesting sight. He became very nervous and jittery as he took my suitcase, putting it in the vehicle and asking me to get in. He took me to a beautiful resort, escorted me to the lobby and asked me to sit and wait, then quickly disappeared.

While sitting there, staff members were coming out from behind doors, looking at me, then disappearing. There were whispers and stares that I just couldn't explain. Finally, a tall gentleman came out of a door behind the front counter, approached me and, in a very thick Aussie accent, said, 'G'day, I'm Peter, the owner. Welcome to Plumes and Arrows. You have certainly caused quite a stir.' When I asked why, he explained that they had never had a single white woman travel to the resort on her own. Other women had come, but usually in groups, so when the booking came in, they had assumed I was a man. It was an interesting start to my three days in Mount Hagen.

I was introduced to my guide, Chris, and told that my tour was about to begin. I wouldn't be staying here at the resort but up in the mountains at an offshoot of the resort called the Tribal Top Inn. As I got in the jeep, there was another man in the back. He was our security, there to look after the vehicle when we stopped and were out of it. I was pretty sure they were concerned for my safety and started wondering what I had gotten myself into.

On the way to the Tribal Top Inn, through the Wahgi Valley and its lush green vegetation, Chris explained the local customs to me while people waved and smiled at us as we passed them on the road. When we arrived at the Inn, I noticed it was surrounded by a massive wooden fence with barbed wire and spikes all around the top. There were security cameras approximately every 20 metres around the fence. Chris pulled up to the security

Family And Career

pad and camera at the entrance, tooted the horn twice, and the massive gate opened. We entered the grounds and the gate was closed behind us.

As we pulled up to what looked like the main reception area, I saw that there were individual huts interspersed around the grounds. After being introduced to Arnel, the manager, and his assistant, Ben, I was shown to my hut. To my surprise, they told me I was going to be the only guest. This was going to be weird as I had booked a number of extras, such as the Wahgi flute players and mud men shows. I was going to be the only one they were performing for!

Next, I was given instructions for the night. Once I was in my hut, I was not to come out for any reason without contacting the reception desk. I was told that they would be letting guard dogs loose on the property at 11 pm as extra security and they would not be able to distinguish a guest from an intruder.

Over the next few days, I saw the most brilliant markets, filled with colourful clothing, fruit and vegetables. I was also a novelty with people stopping to stare and point at me.

All along my journey with Chris, he explained that men in Papua New Guinea were allowed to have more than one wife. The dowry a woman had to bring to the marriage was one pig, he explained. He himself had a couple of wives, but he pointed out that he didn't yet have a white wife. I insisted that I had a boyfriend waiting for me in Australia, hoping that this would put him off. Not only was I unavailable, but I didn't own a pig, I told him, but he continued talking about having a white wife the entire day.

We attended a mock tribal war which was put on for tourists, but in fact, the tribe we were watching had been involved in a war not so long ago. I was shown scars on the men's arms and bodies from the last war, one that had been fought not with guns but with spears.

Afterwards, Chris and I went into one of the huts where all the local village women had gathered. They had me sit on a chair in front of everyone, and Chris started putting a type of red clay on my face, put my hair up and flowers throughout it. When I questioned him, he told me it was just how some women made themselves up as a celebration.

The women were all smiling and clapping their hands together. I have a suspicion that I might have been married that day to Chris in that ceremony. As we drove down the mountain side back to the Tribal Top Inn, everyone who was walking back up the mountain from the markets waved, clapped and smiled at me when they saw me in the jeep with my face and hair done up.

When I entered the Inn and went into the bar, the manager Arnel and the local police chief were there. Both stopped talking immediately, looked at me and asked who had done this to me, the hair and red clay. I told them it was Chris, my guide, after the mock tribal war show, and they suggested that I head to my hut and take it off immediately. But no one would tell me why. Years later, after meeting my husband, Russ, I told him not to be surprised if a black man showed up at our door saying I was his wife and asking for his pig!

The next day, Chris was no longer my guide. Arnel only told me that what he had done was inappropriate and so his assistant Ben was going to be my guide for the remaining time.

That day, we travelled through the Minj Gorge to a village called Kameng, where Ben was from, and I helped prepare a meal with the local villagers. The children were fascinated by my skin colour and my hair, rubbing my arms to see if the colour would rub off and touching my hair constantly.

Later, we headed into the Simbu Province (pronounced Chimbu), where we came across a funeral for a local young man. I was told he had been killed by another tribe because they were jealous that he had gone to Australia and trained as a doctor. The family invited me to sit with them and showed me the burial site, a cave that had skulls lined along one wall. I was told that this area was first settled by German missionaries who introduced Christianity to the locals. It was amazing to see Christianity mixed with local customs, all rolled into one.

That day, as we continued on our journey through the mountains, I saw a python on the side of the road and women carrying massive loads of produce on their heads, walking kilometres to get to market.

Overall, my trip to the island was the most amazing experience I have ever had in a wild and untamed country. But it was time to leave, head back to Australia and continue on my journey.

Return to Australia

Upon my arrival back in Cairns, I decided that I was going to leave Lyn's place. There was a lot of tension between her and her husband, so I headed into town to say goodbye to a couple I had met and spent time with, Alex and Michelle. They were a young couple who lived on a 56' sailboat in the marina at Port Douglas. They told me I couldn't leave yet and insisted I come and stay with them for a few days. They talked me into it, and I ended up staying with them, learning the ropes of the boat, climbing the mizzen in the bosun's chair, swinging from side to side, helping Alex paint different parts of the mast. I spent almost two weeks with them and was extremely grateful for their hospitality, but I felt it was time to continue my journey and head back to Melbourne.

The next part of my trip was with John and Margo, heading across to the west. We went through Adelaide and Ceduna, across the Nullarbor along the Great Australian Bight, through Balladonia and Kalgoorlie.

In Kalgoorlie, I headed to the local cemetery to have a look. I find that cemeteries can tell you a lot about the history of a place. In this cemetery, many infants, some as young as one day old and up to two months old, were buried around the turn of the century, as well as a number of adults. It was obvious that the plague had gone through the community and the most vulnerable had lost their lives.

We then headed up the west coast, past Perth to The Pinnacles, Dongara, Geraldton, Denham, Monkey Mia, Coral Bay, Port Hedland and Broome, Willie Creek, Derby, Fitzroy Crossing, Geikie Gorge and Halls Creek, camping in some wonderful areas. We were able to camp at Purnululu National Park, which was the entrance to the Bungle Bungles. In the camping area were two men who were running a helicopter service for sightseeing around the area. John and Margo decided to gift me a flight for my upcoming birthday, so the following day, we all climbed aboard the helicopter and had a ride through the most amazing landscape I had ever seen, the Bungle Bungles. The area is comprised of beehive-shaped towers made up mostly of sandstone. With orange and dark grey banding around the towers, it actually looks like you are in the midst of huge beehives. The helicopter ride came with the extra bonus of a fixed-wing aircraft flight over Lake Argyle, near Kununurra. So after a few days here, we headed to Kununurra. It was a magnificent area with so much history that went back millions of years.

We stopped at Litchfield National Park and then finally made it to Darwin, where we spent four days. After that stop, we headed down the centre of Australia through Katherine, Mataranka and Daly Waters and into Alice Springs. From there, we went further inland to Kings Canyon, then on to Uluru, where I spent my birthday, and the Olgas. Then, it was on to Coober Pedy, through Port Augusta and Renmark. We finally crossed into Victoria and headed home to Melbourne. What a trip that was! We had completed the western circle of Australia and, while doing that, had met characters from all walks of life.

CHAPTER 15
Unexpected Love

'The beauty of love is that, you can fall into it with the most unexpected person at the most unexpected time.'
~ RITU GHATOUREY

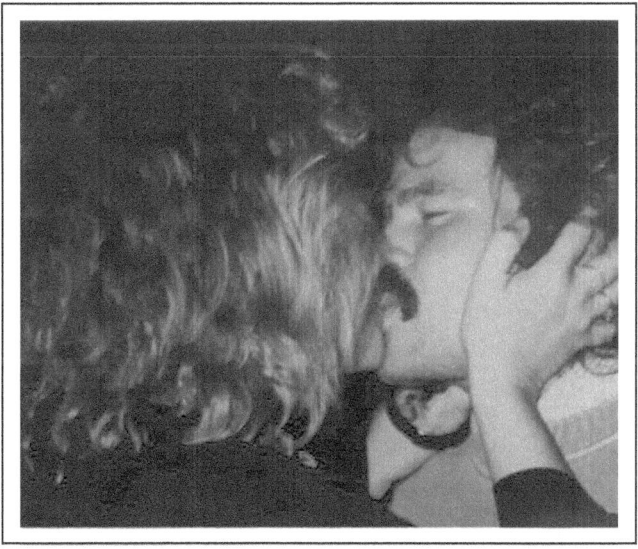

Back in Melbourne life was about to take an unexpected turn. On 14 August 1993, I went to a local 'footy' club with friends. It wasn't the nicest of days. In fact, it had been cold, windy and raining all day. As we sat at the little bar, having a drink, I heard the door open and turned to look. Coming in the door was a guy wearing an Akubra hat, Driza-Bone coat and Blundstone boots, with long curly hair and a full long moustache. He had rain dripping from his hat and looked like he had just come out of the Australian bush. I turned to my friend Tys and said laughing, 'Where did this guy come from? Does he know he's in the city? Where did he leave his horse?' Tys replied, 'Oh, he is harmless. That's Cookie. He's the team manager.' With that, I turned away from the door, not giving him a second thought.

Family And Career

Later, as some of the guys commented about my accent, saying that I was just a frozen Yank, I heard a voice from behind me say, 'That's not an American accent; that's Canadian.' I thought to myself: whoever this is, he's in my good books. I turned and saw that it was Cookie. Then he went about doing what he was doing, and I continued chatting with the other people around me. It wasn't until a couple of days later that I met Cookie again at a pub owned by one of the players.

I was sitting in the lounge with some of the players' wives and girlfriends, while the guys were in the public bar. The bartender came over to me with a drink. As I hadn't ordered one, I asked her where it came from. 'Oh, it's from Cookie,' she said and pointed over to the bar. Cookie was there and smiled, then tipped his hat at me. I can't say what I thought at that point. He seemed such a nice guy but seriously not like anyone I had ever dated or been attracted to. One of the wives sitting with me then said the oddest thing. 'I reckon that one day you and Cookie will be married,' she said. I laughed, completely dismissing it.

Finally, one day, I asked Tys what Cookie's real name was. He told me it was Russell Cooke, but he never used it, just Cookie! Over the next couple of weeks, I swear that everyone was trying to set us up. I was asked to pick Russell up to go to the football. I was asked to give him a ride home. I was asked if I could drop him at work. On top of that, Tys and his girlfriend organised a dinner with me and Russell. The reasons given were numerous, but I did it as something was drawing me to him.

After our dinner with Tys and his girlfriend, I offered Russ a ride home. He directed me to an area in Kew and told me to pull in behind some shops. After parking, he asked if I wanted to come up to his flat for a coffee, and without hesitation, I said, 'Sure.' He lived in a flat above a butcher shop. It was accessed from the rear of the shop through a very large set of wooden stairs. The coffee was made, and we ended up sitting on the lounge room floor, learning an awful lot about each other. He bragged about his children, Bree and Simon, bringing out a photo album, talked about his work and told me about his love of cooking.

Ten days after meeting Russell and driving him to and from his flat, we had gone to the football, then to the pub with everyone afterwards. After having a few drinks, I didn't want to drive so we took a taxi back to his flat and I ended up staying with him. We both felt it was just right. The next day, after finally getting up, we headed back to the pub to pick up my car and stayed for something to eat. All of a sudden, he turned to me, told me he loved me and walked away, looking very sad. On the way back to his flat, I asked him why he looked so sad.

'I promised myself that I would never fall in love or get married again because I have been so badly hurt before,' he replied. 'But I'm in love again and I have spent all afternoon trying to figure out why, and it scares me.'

'If there was a reason for why anything happened, it would be a very dull life,' I said. 'Sometimes, it's just best not to try and figure out why something is happening and just go with the flow.'

I then quoted him one of my favourite sayings: 'To live life in fear is to live half a life.' Needless to say, I ended up staying the night once again. I had never felt so loved by a man, and I was scared I was going to wake up and find it all had been a dream!

I had never really believed in love at first sight, but my thoughts were changing as I had fallen deeply in love with a man I had known less than two weeks. But over the next months, we got to know each other, and we had our ups and downs, the downs because of an ex-girlfriend, but we got through everything.

It came time for me to leave Australia and head back to Toronto and work. My year-long adventure was over, and it was hard to believe. I'd had some amazing experiences, met some incredible people, saw the most amazing country and found a man who I loved with all my heart and who loved me. Leaving

Family And Career

was probably one of the hardest things I have ever had to do. Yes, I was excited about seeing my family, but my heart was staying in Australia with Russell.

The next couple of months were full of emotion, happiness for the birth of my nephew, sadness with the death of a friend and loneliness in missing Russell. But I decided to surprise him for New Year's and fly down for only a couple of days. Yes, everyone thought I was nuts, but I really wanted to see him. I had told him that I would call him at the pub on a certain day and time, but instead, I walked in, not sure of what I would find. He was stunned, looked at me and said, 'You're supposed to ring me!' He then burst into tears and grabbed me in the biggest hug you can imagine. It was a wonderful couple of days before I had to head back. But I knew it wouldn't be for long because Russell had booked a flight to come to Canada for a visit in February.

That month and a half seemed to take forever, but 16 February finally arrived. As I was waiting in the arrivals area of the airport, my heart was beating out of my chest. The anticipation of seeing him again was almost unbearable. I was just hoping that our feelings would be the same as they had been all those months ago. I looked around at all the other people waiting for loved ones and wondered if they were feeling what I was.

As Russell came out the door with his Akubra on his head, wearing just a flannel shirt, jeans and his Blundstone boots, carrying a suitcase, I knew right then that those feelings were still there. With a smile on his face but looking very weary, he said, 'G'day', dropped his suitcase and put his arms around me, and as his lips met mine, I melted. God, it was good to be back with him. I'm sure we were a spectacle in that arrivals area, but I didn't care!

As we finally finished our hellos and were about to walk out into the winter weather, I asked him if he had a coat. It was, after all, −16 degrees Celsius, a beautiful sunny day but what I would call crisp. It had snowed overnight, so it was a pristine white, but very cold! Russell had just come from summer, where it had been 36 degrees, so this was a huge change. He looked at me and cheekily said, 'Yes, my Driza-Bone is in my suitcase, but I'm an Aussie; I'm tough.' With that, I thought I would teach him a lesson, took him by the hand and said, 'Come with me then!'

As we went through the door and out into the cold, I could hear a sharp intake of breath from Russell as he said, 'I think I'll get my coat out.' I replied, 'No, you're a tough Aussie. You can handle it,' and dragged him towards where I had parked. I took my time putting his suitcase in the back as he tried to get in the driver's seat. I asked him if he wanted to drive, but he had forgotten we drove on the other side of the road in Canada. Eventually, I got in the car and leaned over to the passenger side to open his door. When he got in, he said, 'Shit, that's cold!' I don't think he forgot that lesson and was bundled up each time he went out after that.

The next couple of weeks were magical. Russell was introduced to my family, friends, a different country and way of life, especially during the winter. But it went way too fast, and soon, I was taking him back to the airport to send him on his way home. It wasn't a goodbye without tears, but we had put a plan in place where I would apply for residency and hopefully move down to be with him. We had done a lot of talking, and I knew that he didn't want to get married again, but that was okay with me. We didn't have to marry; I just wanted to be with him.

Unfortunately, after a couple months of putting in my papers for residency, I was blatantly turned down as I didn't meet the points required. I was devastated as I even had a job to go to in the security industry. So we decided that I would go down for a short holiday to try and figure out what to do. It was June 1994, and when I arrived, it

Family And Career

was like I had never been gone. The friends I had made all welcomed me with open arms, and Russell was so excited to have me there.

However, a couple of days into my time there, Russell and I had an argument. I'm not even sure what it was about, but I began to question why I was trying to do this, leave my family, the life that I had and relocate to the other side of the world. Margo and I made plans to meet for lunch, but first, I went to Russell's work to let him know. I was still angry with him, and when I said I was going out, he was quiet and just kind of grunted an 'Ok'.

I turned and went to leave, but I heard him mutter something.

Turning back, I said, 'What?'

'Would you marry me?' he repeated.

I was angry and snippily said, 'You know I would. It's you who doesn't want to!' After that, I turned and walked out of the building.

Later that evening, I was having a nap when Russell came into the bedroom and woke me up. I should explain that, since my first visit, he had moved to rooms above the pub.

'Everyone is waiting for us downstairs,' he said.

'Why?' I asked.

'Because I told them I asked you to marry me,' he replied.

I sat straight up in bed, with a stunned look on my face and said, 'You did what!'

'You will, won't you?' he asked, with his head bowed. 'They all want to celebrate with us.'

I just looked at him, astonished, and told him I would be down shortly.

When I got into the pub, where everyone was waiting, no one said a word about the proposal, so I thought he had just said that to get me downstairs. But when his boss went to the bar asking for a bottle of champagne and the publican, Tex, asked what the celebration was for, he said, 'Russ asked Carol to marry him.' Tex started laughing and said, 'Cookie getting married. I don't believe that one.' Everyone knew that Russell never wanted to get married again, so this was certainly a surprise. But even I didn't believe him. There was no ring; it was spur-of-the-moment statement that morning, so why would I believe him?

No one in the group believed him, so he said he was going to phone my father to ask permission. I thought he was joking as he went to the phone to call my dad.

As he dialled each number, I told him, 'Okay, enough is enough. If you do this to my dad and it's a joke, we're over!'

But then the phone rang at the other end, and my dad answered.

'Hi Don, it's Russell here. I have a question to ask you,' he said. 'Can I marry your daughter?'

'Well, I'm okay with that, but have you asked her?' was Dad's reply, I was later told.

'Well, yes, I have, but nobody believes me, so I thought I would call you!' Russell said.

With that, the celebration was on, and the following day, he made it official with a ring. The next days were really a blur, just letting people know and working out what I was now going to do.

I headed home and prepared to work out when I was going to resign.

CHAPTER 16
The End Of An Era

'Every story has an end, but in life every end is a new beginning.'
~ UNKNOWN

When I did decide, after 14 years, to leave the job, it was a decision that I didn't take lightly. It had taken a year of travelling, meeting Russ and coming back to the job to make that decision. It was a secure, well-paying job to which I had given 14 years of my life. It had been exciting, scary, rewarding and even frustrating at times. But policing changes you. You see people at their worst, and you see the things in life that people don't want to see or hear about. It is also a job that people come into and do for years. You don't just step into policing for a couple of years and then step out! It becomes your life and the people you work with, along with other emergency services personnel, become not only your friends but your family. They understand what you do and what you go through, so you bond. They are your lifeline. These were people who had helped shape the person that I had become.

Family And Career

I always thought that I would be in it for life. I was surprised at the disillusionment I felt 12 years into the job and unsure of what to do. I was shocked at my own feelings. I had a fun and exciting career, so when I wasn't sure if I wanted to carry on, I was surprised. I wasn't supposed to feel this way. Dad had been pushing for me to apply for promotion. That's what he had done! People I had come through training with had moved up the ranks, so why wasn't I interested in doing the same? I had been brought up to believe it was noble to have a career, one that lasted a lifetime. At least, that's what I thought I was meant to believe. My dad was very proud that I had followed in his footsteps and believed that the Banks family legacy would continue.

It was because of that, that the hardest thing I had to do was to tell my dad that I was leaving the job for good. You see, Dad always had my back, even though he had no influence in me getting the job in the first place. He had always taught me to be my own person and follow my own path. He was always supportive of whatever role I wanted to take on, and I knew he was proud that one of his children had followed him into the job. To be honest, it was sometimes hard to live up to the legacy of the family, but I did the best that I could. There were times when I hated the fact that I had a family history in the police force — especially a father who was a senior officer. At times, it was put to me by other officers that the only reason I was there was because of him, not because I had worked hard to get my position. That really bothered me, but I was able to prove myself and show others that I deserved to be there.

My sister, Cynthia, had started her own production company called Banks Productions and wanted to do a documentary on my last days on the job. I didn't think the powers that be would let her have access to riding in the car with me, but Chief William McCormack agreed to let it take place.

After getting the platoon on side about this filming, it was set up for Cindy to come out in the car with me and film all facets of my daily job, including time spent with fellow officers. It was a whirlwind of activity in July that year with her filming around 14 Division where I worked, filming the family and riding in the car to calls with me. It was certainly a stressful time for me. Not only did I have to worry for my own safety and that of my partner, but now I had my sister in the car to worry about as well.

The filming went well, and my time on the force was coming to an end. There was only one more thing I wanted to do, and that was to address the Police Services Board, the civilian agency that oversees the Toronto Police Service. I wanted them to know some of the reasons I was so disillusioned with the job. So I asked to be able to make a statement at the public hearing of the board, which is held monthly. It is a private meeting where internal issues are discussed, but there is also a public meeting open to anyone, including the media. The latter was the one I wanted to speak at. I wanted the world to know how tough it was as a young officer right from the proverbial horse's mouth. It took numerous phone calls and requests and even some threats of going to the media, but finally I was granted permission.

This is the last part of the speech I made that day:

'This city has changed dramatically in my 14 years on this force. I have seen people become scared to walk down their streets, scared to say good morning to one another and scared to actually enjoy life. The role of a police officer has become more demanding, more involved and a lot more stressful. Not only are we expected to be law enforcers, but also teachers, social workers, medical caregivers and sometimes, yes, even babysitters. We are expected to be superhuman and, in a life-threatening situation, make a decision in less than five seconds that may haunt us the rest of our lives. When I joined the department, there was compassion. Well, there is no more compassion, just cynicism. After 13 years and 295 days, not that I have been counting, I've had enough and have resigned as of 22 August. I leave with high hopes of a new

Family And Career

and exciting life. But I also leave feeling very sad that a job that I once loved and believed would be my lifelong career is no longer a job I would wish upon anyone. Thank you.'

Then finally at the age of 33, on 22 August 1994, I handed my badge in and ceased to be a police officer, a job I thought would be for life, just like my family before me. With the final packing done and the goodbyes said, I boarded a plane on 31 August 1994 to start a whole new life.

Sitting on the plane about to take off, I had so many emotions running through me. I was excited for the opportunity of a new and interesting life. I was sad that I was leaving my family, new nephew and friends, nervous because I was starting life all over again and scared because I was leaving everything I knew behind. I was joyful to start a new life with Russell, vulnerable because I really didn't know what to expect and hopeful that my new life was exactly what I wanted. As the plane lifted off the ground, I remember looking out the window with tears in my eyes as I said goodbye to my old life and hello to my new one.

This must have been how my grandparents had both felt, taking that first step into a whole new world — my grandfather, when he left Scotland as a boy, and my grandmother, as she boarded a ship from England.

The lesson I took away from them is to take an opportunity when it arises because if you don't, you'll never know what possibilities may await you.

PART 3
A New Life Begins

CHAPTER 17
Unexpected Changes

'If you so choose, even the unexpected setbacks can bring new and positive possibilities. If you so choose, you can find value and fulfilment in every circumstance.'
~ RALPH MARSTON

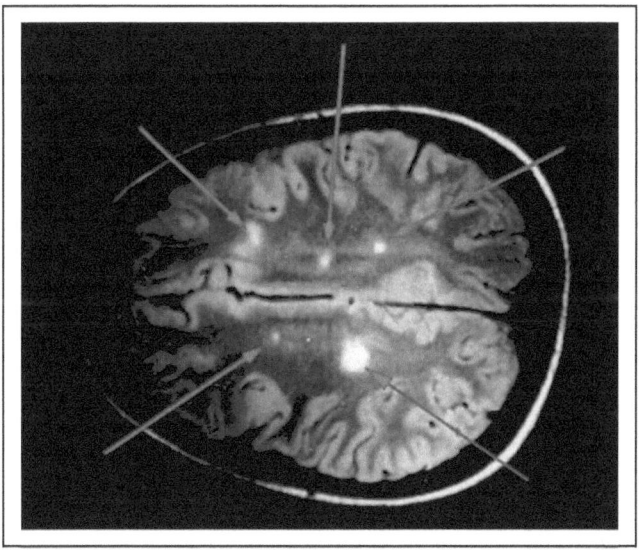

'There are too many lesions on your brain for someone your age, so I have to tell you that you have multiple sclerosis. Basically, your life as you know it is over, so I would suggest you go home and put your affairs in order before you become incapacitated.' The doctor put the big film that he had been looking at up against the ceiling light back into the large envelope in his other hand.

With those two sentences, I felt like I had been hit by a bus.

I said one word that day, sitting in a big armchair in the neurologist's room, 'What?'

'You heard me, you have multiple sclerosis,' he replied, then without a breath continued. 'You will have to quit work, go on

A New Life Begins

a whole bunch of drugs, and this silly sport stuff you do, well, that will have to stop. To be honest, I don't have time for you as a patient. I have enough MS patients already, so you will have to go back to your own doctor.'

He walked to the door, opened it, and said, 'Hurry up. I have patients waiting.'

I think I had to pull my chin off the floor. In a daze, I stood up from the chair with the word 'incapacitated' swirling through my head.

The whole world seemed to go in slow motion as I walked towards the door. With my unknown future in front of me, I approached the doctor, but he slammed the large envelope containing my MRI film into my chest and said, 'See my secretary on the way out.'

'You have got to be kidding!' I thought.

That doctor's office was in a large Victorian terrace house in a leafy suburb of Melbourne. As I walked down the hallway, it became the longest hallway in the world. I walked straight past his secretary's office door, and as my hand reached for the front door handle, I could hear her saying, 'Mrs Cooke, Mrs Cooke, your bill.'

With that, I opened the front door and entered a whole new world.

To this day, I don't remember driving home from that appointment. I know I drove home but have no idea what route I took or how I made it there, nor do I remember parking the car in the carport. The next thing I remember is sitting on the couch in tears, with my six-month-old puppy, Kimba, whimpering, with her head in my lap. This is what snapped me out of my foggy brain.

It was 23 April 1998, 2.15 pm: the date and time of my diagnosis and my introduction to life with multiple sclerosis. In those few hours after that diagnosis, I tried to make decisions that you should never make when faced with trauma. I had been in Australia for four years and married to Russ for three. We had bought a house a year earlier; we were building our life together and I was building a career with Australia Post. I was 'moving up the corporate ladder' as they say and enjoying this fresh start in life. I had made new friends through my involvement in sport, and life was looking pretty good.

Now all I could think of was those words the neurologist had said, that I would become 'incapacitated'. The image I had was of the worst-case scenario, unable to fend for myself, unable to communicate and living in a wheelchair, wearing nappies and drooling. This was not what I had envisioned my life in Australia to be like when I had moved here four years previously. Russ is 10 years older than me, and I couldn't see him having to look after someone 'incapacitated' in our later years, nor would I want to put that burden on him.

That night, when Russ came home from work, I told him what the doctor had said and that I had made some decisions for us. I would give him a divorce, give him the house and go back to Canada to have my family look after me. The true bush-boy Aussie in him bluntly told me I was a 'fucking idiot'. Then he explained that we knew nothing about this disease. That I didn't have it, we had it — him and I — and we would deal with it once we were armed with more information. We needed to learn more so we could deal with what might happen in the future. I am one of the luckiest people on earth because I have someone in my corner accepting me for who I am, through the good and the bad times.

What we did learn, after consulting my family doctor, was that multiple sclerosis is a disease of the central nervous system involving the brain, the spinal cord and the optic nerves. It is an autoimmune disease where the body thinks that there is something wrong with the myelin, the fatty substance that surrounds and protects our nerves, so the body attacks it. This causes areas of scar tissue or sclerosis, called lesions, on the myelin, so that when a message is travelling through the nerve, it gets to a break and stops, thinking it's not safe to pass. The message, therefore, doesn't get to where it is supposed to go.

This can cause a number of different symptoms depending on where in the body the nerve is. Symptoms may include vision problems, balance and coordination issues, dizziness, difficulty thinking clearly, numbness and tingling, fatigue, stiff muscles, bowel or bladder problems, pain or paralysis and many more. I also learned that no two people are alike when it comes to MS. We may all experience similar symptoms but never exactly the same.

There are also several different types of MS:

• Relapsing and remitting, which means that eventually the myelin will repair itself and the symptoms will disappear.

• Progressive, which means that there is no repair of the myelin and the symptoms continue to worsen.

• Secondary Progressive, which means that after a number of years of relapsing and remitting the myelin cannot repair itself anymore, so progression of symptoms happens.

I was on the lucky end of the scale in that I was diagnosed with Relapsing and Remitting MS.

Now, if I hadn't been born pig-headed and stubborn or hadn't been taught to question things, that diagnosis, especially delivered the way it was, could have been the last day of my life. Instead, it started a journey of understanding not only how to deal with symptoms but also how to deal with living life a different way. I was bound and determined that I would continue to work and do the sport that I loved. It was definitely a negative change in life at the start, and it probably took me a good year to try and change my way of thinking.

Eventually, it was like a switch had been flipped on in my head. I decided that I had MS but it did not have me, and I wanted to live with it, not fight it. I decided that the neurologist was right: my life as I knew it was over. But he was thinking in a negative way, and I decided it was going to be in a positive way. I was determined that MS was not going to define who I was. This didn't happen overnight. It was, and sometimes still is, a constant struggle to learn how to live with it and incorporate it into my life.

My goal as a teenager was always to represent my country at the highest level of sport, and although that goal hadn't happened, I always had the notion that I was meant for something bigger. What it was, I wasn't sure, but boy I wasn't expecting it to be MS. I had never been sick; I had always been healthy and fit, tried to do the right things and be the best version of myself I could be, so why me?

But through gathering knowledge, I found the answer to that question. I realised that, although MS is one of the most common neurological conditions in young adults and almost everyone I meet knows someone with MS, none of them seem to know what it is. So I decided that having the ability to educate, inspire and advocate about living with this condition would be my answer to this question.

Life continued on pretty much as it had before my diagnosis. I continued to work with bouts of hospital stays when I would have a relapse. But most of my bosses throughout my career with Australia Post were pretty good, letting me work from home if I needed to. I continued to swim with the Masters club that I had been with, and I was still competing.

I had always thought that I would fight this disease by not ever using mobility aids, but in 2001, I realised that if I wanted to keep my independence I would have to use a wheelchair. This is when my real introduction to disability began. I recognised that this wasn't giving in to the disease but living with it by using an aid. I was also having a lot of relapses, and each time I was recovering, I was stressed about getting back to work, which was causing me to relapse again. So I made probably the most important decision of my life, to leave full-time employment. I was scared. This was not in my life plan, but the stress certainly wasn't helping my health. I can look back now and see that, in fact, it was probably the best decision I ever made. I was able to concentrate on me and not worry about getting back to work to please others.

A New Life Begins

Over the next few years, my health was up and down, but I was able to get out of the wheelchair and walk again thanks to the intervention of an amazing rehabilitation doctor, John Olver. He was using Botox to stop messages from the nerves to the muscles in order to retrain the muscles to work properly. This treatment option was expensive and not covered by Medicare, so he said he would use me to train other doctors on how to administer the drug. I decided to give it a try.

With injections into my leg, very intensive physiotherapy and more injections six months later, I was able to get out of the chair. I also started to exercise more, which not only helped strengthen my legs but gave me a boost of positivity. I thank John Olver for giving me this chance to walk again.

Just before I had left full-time work, I had run an event called the 24 Hour Mega Swim. It was a team event that sought to raise money for the MS Society of Victoria to help fund a program called the 'Go for Gold Scholarships'. These scholarships enabled people living with MS to follow a dream. As I was working on walking again, I felt like I needed to have a purpose, and the 24 Hour Mega Swim was it. So, an event that was supposed to be a one-off became my saviour and an annual event.

My health issues didn't stop once I was walking. MS decided to attack my bowel function, and after numerous interventions, including an ileostomy, I ended up having to have a total colectomy. This was major surgery and a huge decision. I could try having the small bowel connected to the rectum muscle and hope it took over for the large missing bowel, or I could go with a colostomy bag the rest of my life. I took the punt connecting the small bowel, and it worked! The surgery was a success but not without its problems. I ended up with Multi Resistant Staph Infection (MRSI) in my incision, having to have blood transfusions and feeling so bad that I didn't think I could get through it.

Unexpected Changes

While trying to recover from the infection, I was approached by the head of the hospital and the nurse in charge on my surgical ward with some news. I wasn't feeling the best as they made their way into my hospital room. I wondered what was going on and was concerned that the head of the hospital was visiting. They explained that some error had occurred with the cleaning of a tray of instruments used during my surgery.

There had been an issue with the tape that goes across the tray, which is supposed to change colour after each cleaning phase to indicate that it has gone through that process. The tape colour had been changed prematurely on two trays, one of which was mine. This meant that the tray had not been put through the final deeper cleaning phase, which ensured that cylindrical instruments were clean on the inside.

What did this mean for me? I was told that no cylindrical instruments had been used in my surgery. Still, because the tray hadn't gone through its final phase, it was suggested I have an HIV test done in a few months' time. Not exactly what I wanted to hear and just something more to add to the stress levels at the time.

I demanded that my husband and mother not be told and that no one, not one nurse, was to be talking about this on the floor. I wanted to be the one to tell them. They were stressed out enough as it was because of the surgery, the infection and my body's MS response to the surgery. There was nothing we could do about this right now, and I just wanted to get through these first steps, then deal with the HIV issue.

My surgeon came in to see me and assured me that he hadn't used any instruments that would have been affected. But to be honest, this did nothing for the worry that was running through my head at the time. I didn't say anything to my family until I was well and truly in rehabilitation and getting my life back on track. But by then, I wasn't sure how to tell Russ and needed to use the hospital psych to talk through how to let him know. When I did let both Russ and Mom know, it was okay because I had my head around it as well.

A few months later, I did have the HIV test and all came back ok. I did get through the surgery and infection but had to learn to walk all over again as my MS had kicked in due to the stress of the surgery. The resilience I gained from going through these tough times has helped me over the years to deal with other issues in life.

As my dad taught me, you must constantly gather knowledge to gain wisdom to be skilful. Finding out all I could after my MS diagnosis gave me the wisdom to be skilfully living the best way possible with it. Without this knowledge, I would most likely be living a life ruled by a chronic disease. It also helped equip me to deal with the other health issues in my life and taught me not to panic, to take each issue as it came, gain knowledge and just take it step by step.

CHAPTER 18

One Life — Live It

*'Don't be afraid of death; be afraid of an unlived life.
You don't have to live forever, you just have to live'*
~ NATALIE BABBITT

Throughout my life, I have learned through the sadness of losing people that we must live each day as if it's our last. When I lost my grandfather at the age of 12 and then a couple of friends during high school, one to suicide and two to car accidents, it brought home to me that life was indeed precious.

My own experience with possible death occurred in 1982 when my sister and I were on our first holiday by ourselves, without parents, in Florida. We had met other holiday goers, and on one particular night, I decided to go out with them while Cindy stayed in the hotel. It was a very late night, and after being out on the town, there were about eight of us in one of the guys' hotel room, drinking coffee for a few hours. At about 5 am, I decided that I had

A New Life Begins

better head back to my hotel, which was only about a kilometre down the road, said my goodbyes and headed out the door.

One of the young guys, Mike, called out to me and offered me a ride. He didn't want me walking in the dark. Mike was a British sailor on his way home from the Falklands War. His ship had docked in Fort Lauderdale, and he was on two weeks' furlough with a few of his work colleagues. We hadn't been drinking for hours, so I decided to say yes to the offer. I opened the passenger door, slid into the passenger seat and didn't put my seatbelt on. I figured it was such a short trip down the road it wouldn't be needed.

As we headed down the road, Mike leaned across the bench seat to change the radio station, and as he did, he turned the steering wheel causing the car to hit the curb. I think he panicked and hit the gas pedal instead of the brake and we sped up right into a light pole. I still remember it vividly. It comes back to me in slow motion, me yelling about the pole and then nothing. The lights went out.

I'm not sure how long I was out, but when I came to, there was blood everywhere; my eyes were swelling fast, which was making it hard to see. I found out later that my face had hit the windshield. Everything hurt. My arms, my chest, my leg. I tried to get out of the car but I couldn't; there was something between me and the passenger door. I tried to look over at Mike, but I couldn't see what had happened to him; there was too much blood running down my face.

Eventually, emergency services arrived, and I remember a paramedic beside me at the window telling me to relax, close my eyes and they would get me out. I had this overwhelming feeling that if I closed my eyes they wouldn't open again, so I fought the urge to do so and stayed conscious throughout my extraction out of the car. It took a while as I had to go out through the driver's door.

When I hit the window, my chest had made a huge dent in the dashboard. I was told later that I was lucky I didn't have my seatbelt on. After hitting the dash and window, I had bounced back into the middle of the car's bench seat as the engine came through the passenger side of the car. The engine was between me and the passenger side door. Had my seatbelt been on, I'd be dead.

Part of the engine had gone through the front of my right leg beside the shin bone. My right arm was broken, and I had been partially scalped with the centre front of my hair left in the window where my head had gone through. I had a huge amount of glass in my face, chest and hands. It took years to get out. But I had survived.

Mike survived too but didn't make it back to his ship and had to be flown home weeks later. He had broken almost everything on his left side as he hit the steering wheel, actually sheering it off. He had just been fighting a war with not a scratch on him, but after that drive, he was a mess. I must add a note that he was tested for alcohol and it came back negative. He just panicked when he hit the curb.

As I didn't have insurance for hospital cover, they charged me for everything. I had 25 stiches across my face, between my eyes, which they charged per stitch. They wouldn't plaster my arm but put it in a splint, which I had to have re-broken and set at home. They didn't stitch up my leg, hence my round scar now, and wouldn't keep me in the hospital even though I had a major head injury. It was left up to my 19-year-old sister to look after me in a hotel room.

We couldn't get the airline to change our flight, so it wasn't the best situation, but I realised what compassion is all about as the hotel staff, local restaurants and guests helped us as much as they could. Everyone was amazing. Even a couple from Toronto, who were on holidays, came to see if there was anything they could do. The couple had contacted the police to find out where I was, after the crash had made the paper. Turns out that they were both associated with the Toronto Police Force and he worked in the area right beside where I was working at the time.

A New Life Begins

Once I was home and on the mend, I was certainly grateful for life! I knew that I was so lucky not to have died or been more seriously injured, and I vowed that day to live life to the fullest. I also learned that if you go to the United States for holidays, make sure you have the top travel insurance to cover hospital!

My second experience with near death occurred in 2003, right after my bowel surgery.

I was in rehabilitation, getting my body working again, and I had pain in my lower right abdomen. My bowel surgeon was called in, thinking that it had to do with the surgery I had just been through. As it turned out, I had a growth on my right ovary, so back into surgery to remove the ovary, which was a little setback on the road to recovery. But the pathology came back good, and eventually, after three months in hospital, I made it home in one piece, although missing a few pieces!

A few months later, after a quick trip home to Canada to surprise my sister for a belated 40th birthday celebration, the pain returned. This time, it was in the lower left of my abdomen. I didn't say anything while in Canada, but as soon as I got home, I saw my doctor. I was sent off to see a gynaecologist, who ordered some tests and said he would call me with the results. I hadn't heard anything from him after a week, so I called his offices and asked his receptionist if my test results were back. After putting me on hold, she came back on the line and said she had just looked at them and they were all fine.

On Friday 31 October 2003, I remember it well, I received a call from the doctor, saying he had my results back. When I told him his receptionist had already told me they were clear, you could hear him hesitate and say that she was wrong and shouldn't have told me anything.

He then proceeded to say, 'Your blood tests reveal that marker levels are high, pointing to ovarian cancer, and there are more growths on your left ovary. So I would like you not to worry but to come in and see me first thing next Wednesday.'

One Life — Live It

Not to worry! Don't you love it when they tell you that it might be ovarian cancer but not to worry!

Wednesday the following week was the earliest he could see me because it was Melbourne Cup week, a horse race that stops the nation and is a public holiday in Melbourne. Even though the race was on the Tuesday, everything would be closed the Monday. It was a very long weekend trying not to worry!

As Russ and I made our way to his offices on the Wednesday, there wasn't a lot said between the two of us, each lost in our own worlds and thoughts. I think he was probably more worried than me as I was looking at it as just another hiccup. As soon as the doctor called us into his office, he sat down, looked at the paperwork and said he wanted to send us upstairs to see a colleague of his, a gynaecology oncologist, who would be better equipped to handle my case. Well, this didn't sound too good.

We headed up the lift into the offices of Mr Robert Rome, and I approached the receptionist telling her I needed to make an appointment. Her reply was that the first available one would be in the new year. I told her that information had been faxed up from downstairs. She turned to look at the fax, pulled some papers, read them, looked at her computer, looked at me and said, 'How about tomorrow at 2.15 pm?' It was then I knew that this was serious.

Thursday morning arrived, and I told Russ that I would go to the appointment on my own. I figured that the worst thing Mr Rome could tell me was that I needed more surgery. Sure enough, that is exactly what he said. After looking at my test results and an examination, he asked me what I was doing the following week.

'I'm guessing, seeing you at a hospital somewhere,' I replied.

I asked him if he was just taking the other ovary out, and he told me that no, it would be a full hysterectomy. I kind of giggled to myself thinking that there wasn't going to be a lot of organs left inside of me if I kept this up.

A New Life Begins

I think he was surprised at my 'matter of fact' attitude; I just was down to business wanting to know the procedure and lots of information. I had learned from my MS diagnosis that I needed knowledge before my brain kicked in with 'what if' scenarios.

As I left the appointment, it was like the world had sped up and my head was spinning. I had things that I needed to cancel and plans to put in place before the surgery the following week. I wasn't panicked; I was just trying to take it step by step. I also realised that this stress of surgery would probably send my MS into overdrive again, and I wanted to be prepared.

The following week, as I was prepped for surgery in my second hospital for the year, I was pretty calm and trying to remain positive. I believe that having dealt with the trauma of being diagnosed with a chronic illness in the past was helping me deal with this illness in the present. It was definitely going to be a step-by-step process, surgery first, the rest later.

The surgery went fine and the pathology came back good. This was a huge relief, but again, my body decided not to work due to the stress and my MS, so the day arrived when I was going to be transferred by to the rehab hospital. As I was getting ready, I ended up having a huge haemorrhage, and with blood everywhere, I was taken back into surgery. I had lost so much blood that, again, I was given a blood transfusion and, again, I ended up with MRSI. But this time it was much worse, and I was so sick that my mom flew in, once again, from Canada, hoping for the best but thinking the worst.

It was probably the first time in my life where I was so sick I wanted it to end. I was almost at my limit and didn't want to go through any more. The only drug that combats MRSI is called Vancomycin, and it makes you sick before it makes you better. It caused me to continually vomit, caused flushing of my upper body and made me feel extremely unwell. At times, I couldn't tell if it was the infection or the drug causing the problems.

Eventually, the drugs started to kick in, and I slowly started to feel better, but certainly not before I had those feelings of wanting it to just end. This year had just been too much for me, and I felt like I was done fighting; yet something in me refused to give up. I felt like I still had a lot to accomplish in life. I believe that it was Russ, my sister via phone, friends who never gave up on me, and my mom who was by my side almost 24/7, who pulled me through that tough experience.

I was finally able to head back to rehab to continue on my road to recovery. It was certainly a long year, and I even had Christmas and New Year's in hospital with a day trip home on Christmas to give me a taste of what was to come … home.

Over the next year, there were a few health issues to contend with due to this last surgery. I had been having kidney infections, which were putting me in hospital and were something I had never had before. It looked like I had a fistula between the bladder wall and the small bowel. So it was once again into surgery, with my bowel surgeon and my urologist working together. It was possible that I would end up with a colostomy bag for the rest of my life and just one more thing to deal with. But I went into the surgery with a positive attitude.

I was right to be positive. It turned out that a stitch from my previous surgery hadn't dissolved and was stuck on the outside wall of my bladder. It had caused scar tissue, which had eaten through the wall of the bladder and was causing bacteria to develop through the bladder, turning into kidney infections. The surgeons were able to take this foreign material out, and it solved all the issues.

These couple of experiences built in me the resilience to get through anything. It taught me that, if we remain positive, we can overcome anything. Getting through one trauma in life can equip you with tools to get you through another one. I was going to get back out and try to live life to the fullest.

CHAPTER 19

Chasing Dreams

*'If you can imagine it, you can achieve it.
If you can dream it, you can become it.'*
~ WILLIAM ARTHUR WARD

I remember it well. It was 1968; I was seven years old, and I was watching amazing girls doing gymnastics on television at the Mexico Olympics. I had been doing gymnastics for a couple of years, and after watching this spectacle, I decided then and there that I wanted to be a gymnast at the Olympics, representing Canada. It was all I thought about.

At the age of nine, my best friend, Sharon, and I decided that we were going to try out for the Winstonettes Gymnastics Club. This was my first foray into 'elite' sport. As we arrived at the tryouts, I was so excited. There were lots of girls who seemed to have the same dream as me. I remember standing before a woman at the registration desk, who asked my name, measured my height, then made me stand on the scales to take my weight. She looked at me and told me that I was too fat and the wrong body type to be a gymnast. I wasn't allowed to try out for the club. That was it. My tryout was over, and I hadn't even shown them what I could do!

I was devastated. No one had ever told me that I was too fat before, and to make matters worse, as I sat and watched the tryouts, Sharon was asked to join the club. With my dreams in tatters, I headed home with Sharon and her mother. Upon arriving home, I ran into my room in tears, slamming the bedroom door behind me. My mom came in to find out what was going on, and after telling her what the woman had said, she had one good piece of advice for me.

'If you want to do gymnastics, don't let anyone tell you not to. Just do it. If you want to go to the Olympics, then maybe you should try another sport,' Mom said.

Wow! I had never thought about doing another sport, my mother was teaching me to think outside the box. If the way you're doing something isn't working, then try it a different way. This was a lesson I took throughout my life. Unfortunately, as children, our beliefs are formed through our association with the world around us, and that woman telling me I was too fat started a very long road to learning to love my body type. It took me about 40 years. Although I struggled with my body self-esteem, I didn't let it stop me from getting into other sports, and I have my mother to thank for that.

I continued to do gymnastics because I loved it and actually did it right up into high school, representing my school in local competitions. I did eventually realise that I didn't have the build to be an elite gymnast, but I still loved doing it anyway.

My sister and I had been involved in many sports growing up. My parents had enrolled us in learn to swim programs from a young age. So at the age of ten, I decided that I wanted to try competitive swimming and joined a local swim club, the Scarborough Dolphins Swim Club. I loved it!

My first swim meet was held away from our home pool. My first race that day was the 50-yard freestyle. I swam my heart out, came fifth and was presented with a green ribbon. I looked over at the first-place winner's ribbon, which was a beautiful red colour. From that day, I decided that I wanted red ribbons, not green, so my swimming career started in earnest.

By the time I was 15, I was training twice a day during the week. I was at the pool by 5.30 am every morning before school, and every evening at 6 pm, with another session on Saturday mornings. I was obsessed with being the best I could be, and it was paying off. I was swimming well.

It was 1976 and the Montreal Olympics were being held in Canada. There was such excitement around the country, and I consumed every newspaper article I could find on the Canadian team. I plastered my bedroom wall with newspaper clippings, so I could see them every morning as I woke up and every night as I went to sleep. I decided that my goal would be to represent Canada at the 1980 Moscow Olympics.

This life was a tough slog. Mom and Dad made sure that I kept my marks up at school and told me I needed to have a part-time job. I was supposed to make some money to help them pay for all my swimming, so I got a job working a few hours a week at a pizza place. I don't think they ever asked me for any of the money that I made, but it certainly was teaching me that good things don't happen for free. I had to work to be a good swimmer, but I also had to work to show that I was serious about doing this.

Unfortunately, as we got closer to 1980, athletes across the Western world realised that the games wouldn't be happening because of politics. It was a nightmare for all of us. I will never know if I would have made the team. Regardless, it was a dream that was taken away from me through no fault of my own.

As I grew up, moving on from school into the workforce, I always felt that there was something missing. That goal I had

had my whole life growing up still burned bright in my soul. In 1985, when I found out that the first World Police and Fire Games would be taking place, I felt like this was my opportunity to shine. I could represent my force and my country at the highest level for me at that time. Along with hundreds of emergency personnel from around the world, I flew to San Jose, California, to compete. I came away with a number of medals, but more importantly, I made friends from Australia who would become instrumental in my travels 'down under' in the future.

I was still swimming competitively as a Masters swimmer in Australia when I was diagnosed with multiple sclerosis. Actually, it was at the Australian Masters Championships when my symptoms hit me full on.

I thought I was going to have a really good competition. I was ready. I had trained really well and was looking forward to racing. Instead, I swam like a rock. I felt like I had the flu coming on. I spent a few days in bed after arriving home and wasn't feeling much better. I was so lethargic; my balance was off, and then I started having double vision, as though my eyes were shaking from side to side. My husband assured me that they weren't from his point of view, but I couldn't focus on anything, and it gave me a feeling of constant sea sickness.

I decided to get my eyes tested and went to see the local optometrist, a young woman who had just graduated from university. She conducted a number of tests and then had me do a field vision test. It was like playing a kind of computer game where I had to push a button each time I saw a little red dot. Unfortunately, I failed the test very badly on my left eye, not seeing any of the red dots in my peripheral vision. When I told her that my doctor thought I had an inner ear infection, she told me that it might have infected the eye as well and asked for his name and phone number. She informed him that I had optic neuritis, which is a precursor to MS, and asked to have me tested.

Chasing Dreams

It was then that my doctor sent me to the neurologist who eventually diagnosed me. But I decided that I would live with MS and continue with my life. So I kept swimming.

In 2005, the World Masters Games were going to be held in Edmonton, Canada, and for the first time ever, they were going to have Para events in swimming and athletics. I decided to see if I could qualify as a Para-swimmer. I was classified as an S10 swimmer and competed at the games, bringing home six gold and one silver medal.

Towards the end of 2005, the Australian Paralympic Committee (APC), as they were known then, invited me to a Talent Search Day. I was very surprised as I thought such days were aimed at young disabled athletes to encourage them to take up sport so they could become future Paralympians. It later dawned on me that the APC had no idea how old I was. I was 44 at the time, but I went anyway.

I was about 24 years older than the oldest athlete there, but I went through all the testing with them. About three weeks later, I received a letter asking me to take up rowing, a new sport for the Beijing 2008 Paralympic Games for which I had apparently showed potential. Rowing? I was used to being in the water, not on top of it!

No matter what your age is, if you have a dream, you can still go for it! Age shouldn't be a barrier and shouldn't stop you from attaining your goals.

CHAPTER 20
Life As A Rower

'Fall in love with the process and the results will come.'
~ SEAN MCCABE

To be honest, it probably took me four months to find a rowing club that would take me on. I made the mistake, when I called the clubs, of telling them that I had a slight disability, and every single one of them told me they couldn't help me. The word 'disability' scares people. Instead of asking me what the problem was, they shut me down. That was until I reached the Yarra Yarra Rowing Club, right in the heart of Melbourne.

The young man who answered my call was the first person to ask me what my slight disability was.

'Do you think you can get in the boat?' he asked, after I told him I had MS.

'Well, I can probably get in, but I might need help getting out,' I replied.

A New Life Begins

He told me to come down to the club and that they were having a 'Learn to Row' course starting the following week. Talk about timing. It was great!

That was the start of a new sporting career. I'm not sure I loved it straight away. It was and is the toughest sport I think I have ever done. You have to be aware of your whole body, use your brain constantly and go backwards. Simply trying to keep everything moving is exhausting. There is no rest. Unfortunately, shortly after doing the course, I had a pretty substantial MS relapse, which put me in hospital. This time, it had affected both my arms and legs, so I was back into rehab, learning to reuse everything. At the end of November 2006, as soon as I could, I was back at the club, back in the boat and learning to row once again.

In January 2007, I contacted Rowing Australia to find out what I had to do to get on the Australian team for the 2008 Beijing Paralympics. I was told that I would have to compete at the national championships. I just assumed they meant in 2008, but no, they meant in March 2007. God, I had just learned to row!

I asked what type of boat I had to row in, and the reply was either a single or a double. The single was out. Although I had tried to row a single scull, I kept falling into the Yarra River. My swimming skills certainly helped there! So, the double it would have to be. And I was allowed to row with a non-disabled rower.

A young woman by the name of Fiona Munn offered to partner with me. She had been rowing for a number of years and was very experienced. The only problem was that my sister and her children were coming to Australia to visit and I had planned a trip to the centre of Australia with them, returning to Melbourne only a few days before the championships. So our training was one of quality, not quantity, and done while my family was visiting, before our trip into central Australia. Fiona and I worked well together.

Saturday 10 March 2007 arrived quickly. I was heading to Nagambie, Victoria, for my first ever Australian Rowing Championships, with

Fiona and her husband. To say I was nervous is an understatement! Our boat had been taken up by the club trailer, and once we got there, we just had to make sure the set-up was right for us.

As it came time to head to the start, we had help putting our boat in the water and I took my place in the 'stroke' seat. This is the designated seat for the disabled rower, which also sets the stroke rate for the boat. The officials wanted to see how the disabled rower handled this, with the able-bodied rower following them, sitting in the bow seat.

I was so nervous. It was mid-afternoon, and the sun was out in full force with a slight headwind running down the course. I was sweating, but it was more from my nerves than from the heat. I had done some other races on the Yarra River in the lead-up to this, but this was such a bigger scale. I just wanted to remember what I was supposed to do. My head was a jumble of information, with the start sequence, the body sequence of actually rowing and just hoping I didn't 'catch a crab', flipping us into the water! Catching a crab occurs when the rower's blade gets trapped in the water by the momentum of the shell, and the oar handle flies backwards, going over the rower's head or striking the rower's chest. Often, the handle ends up behind the rower. In extreme cases, the rower may be thrown overboard. It's called 'catching a crab', and sooner or later, it happens to everyone.

We made our way to the start line, where our competitors were lining up as well. The past national champion was in the middle lane. Fiona and I were to their right, with the other boat to their left. With the wind, it was hard to keep the boat straight and in line with the other boats, but eventually the gun went off, and away we went. Fiona was great in keeping me focused on what I had to do. She kept my head in the game, staying calm and giving me direction on what I should be doing.

We had 1,000 metres to row, and with only a few wobbles, we made it down the course, surprisingly crossing the line in 4:37.78

A New Life Begins

minutes and well ahead of the other two crews. I couldn't believe it: we had won! Once we crossed the line, I felt like my body was on fire. I had never worked so hard in my life and, in my first ever Double Scull race, had taken out the national title. I felt like I was on my way to making the team for Beijing. I knew I had a long, long way to go, but at least I had accomplished the first step!

Our club was elated for their first national championships win. Everyone on the banks of the rowing course were yelling and screaming with excitement. They wanted to celebrate, and all I felt like doing, even in my excitement, was lie down and let the blood flow back into my legs!

I was excited. If I could accomplish this after a month of training, think what I could do in a year. This dream of mine might come true. This was just going to spur me on.

A few months later, I saw an advertisement on the Rowing Australia website for athletes to come to Canberra to get properly classified. So I sent an email to the 'Adaptive Rowing' (as it was called then) coordinator to ask if I should be going to Canberra to get classified. I waited a few days, only to receive a response that was disgusting. If I had been a 17-year-old getting into a new sport, I would have quit, but because I was a 46-year-old woman who was pig-headed and stubborn, I just got angry.

In his email, the coordinator stated that, after having watched me row at the nationals, he believed that I would never be good enough or fit enough to make a national team. Point blank, that was it. Thoughts of when I was nine years old came back! No one was going to tell me what I could and couldn't do. How dare he think he could decide for me! He had no idea the drive and determination that was inside me. I took three days to compose a response. Not only did I send it to him, I sent it to his boss, the CEO of Rowing Australia, the CEO of Rowing Victoria and my own personal coach.

I told him very politely where he could stick his email, that he didn't know me and how dare he judge a book by its cover. I told

Life As A Rower

him that this was not the best way to entice new rowers to the sport. I wrote that I had only been rowing for about a month and knew I had a long way to go but that I would show him what I was made of. I also told him that I would be going to Canberra to get classified whether or not he thought I should.

Within a week, I received an email from Rowing Australia inviting me, all expenses paid, to Canberra for the classification and to take part in a rowing camp for three days. When you stick up for yourself, it's amazing what you can accomplish.

The next year was an incredible year of learning. I did go to the classification, came away with the classification of LTA (Legs, Trunk and Arms rower) and met some incredible people who became very good friends. I spent the year training hard, not only with crews but also, finally, in a single. This time, I managed to stay in and not fall into the Yarra River. And in February 2008, at the Sydney International Regatta Centre (SIRC), I was part of a group of LTA rowers vying for a seat in the coxed four, a four-person rowing boat, to race at a World Cup in Germany. Another step toward the Beijing Paralympics.

I remember sitting in the rowing sheds at SIRC. I was waiting to hear the outcome of the trials. The outcome would determine if Rowing Australia thought that we were good enough to send a crew to the World Cup, and if so, who would be in that crew. The anticipation sent little nervous flutters running through my stomach. The coach stood up and said that the boat had a long way to go, that those who made it would have to work hard, but they did want to send a boat to the World Cup. I was so excited. It was like what I imagine waiting for the answer on a game show would be like. You just want them to hurry up and tell you! Finally, the crew was named, and I was in it! The relief was overwhelming. I'd taken a second step forward. All we had to do was qualify. Then, we would be on our way to Beijing, and my dream would be fulfilled!

At the end of April, the crew, consisting of myself, Brandie O'Connor, Pete Siri, Gene Barrett and Lisa Brown, our coxswain,

A New Life Begins

headed to our last camp at SIRC before going to Germany. We were finally getting it together and rowing pretty well, so things were looking up. We were all positive; there was no thought of not making it to Beijing. Most of the qualifying had been done at the last World Championships, and there were only three spots left. Two boats would go through from the final at the World Cup, first and second place, with one wild card boat to go through. We were sure we would get one of those spots.

A few days before leaving for Germany with the rest of the team, we were presented with our team clothing. It was so exciting to be part of such an amazing team, and I was in awe of some of the rowers I had as teammates. At 46, I was on my first Australian team and heading overseas. Others might not have believed I could do it, but I did!

It was so exciting to get to the rowing centre outside of Dachau, not far from Munich, and be surrounded by rowers from countries around the world. This was the last chance for some of these crews to make the cut for the Olympics and Paralympics, so the tension in the air was thick. We had three days to get ready for our heat and the race for lanes. There were only five countries in the Para program aiming for those remaining three spots: Japan, China, South Africa, Denmark and us.

Race day arrived, and the nerves within our crew were showing. Gene was the only one in the boat who had ever raced at this level. As we were rowing to the start, things just didn't feel good in the boat. Thankfully, our coxswain, Lisa, was doing a great job of keeping us focused and trying to lower the tension, saying that we knew what we had to do and had practised this. It was also only about the third time we had ever started with our boat being held at the start gates. Usually, we just had to keep the boat straight without it being held by an actual person or gate, so it was a little weird having the end of it held.

Life As A Rower

We settled as we waited for the start, then the start beep went. We had the worst start I think we ever had, and that put us off for the entire race! We did everything wrong: rushing the slide, no drive from the legs, with some of us looking around and not concentrating on what we should be doing, instead focusing on where the other boats were. We crossed the line in fourth place. Thank god, this was only the race for lanes for the final.

We had to go back and debrief about what had happened. We were unfocused, and I think that was because it was our first time competing at this level. I was sure that we would get it together for the final. We sat with the coaches and talked about the race, what had gone wrong and what we could do better.

Two days later, on Saturday 10 May 2008, we headed back to the regatta centre for the final. I knew we were nervous because of our performance in the heats, but we were all optimistic that we were going to do well. We had probably the best start ever, coming together like a well-oiled machine. Lisa was directing us with precision, and at the 500-metre mark, we were in second place. Lisa called for another push. I could feel the boat surge forward, concentrated on Pete's back and drove my legs as hard as I could. With 50 metres to go, I could feel the boat slightly slowing. We had nothing more to give, even though Lisa was yelling at us to 'drive' and 'dig deep'.

I was absolutely spent when I heard the beep as our bow ball went across the finishing line. I was just trying to suck in as much air as I could. My legs were on fire, and I felt like I was going to throw up. We had no idea where we had placed. All Lisa could tell us was that China had won, but it had been a blanket finish for 2nd, 3rd and 4th. We sat there in agony as we waited for the photo finish to be put up on the screen. The photo went up with literally the three boats, us, Denmark and South Africa, crossing together. Now it was down to the times.

A New Life Begins

As the results flashed up on the big screen, I wanted to cry. We had placed fourth. But between second and fourth place, there was only 0.8 seconds. Denmark had come second so were on their way to Beijing. Now we had to wait for the decision to be made about the last wild card place, and unfortunately for us, South Africa won that. That was likely because Australia already had a couple of boats in other categories and South Africa had none.

We rowed towards the docks, and as we got there, I realised that I couldn't get out of the boat. My legs had given up and I had nothing left in them, so the coaches lifted me out of the boat, telling me that they would go get a wheelchair for me. I declined and told them I just wanted to lie on the dock for a few minutes and see if they would start working again. They left me to my own world, and as I lay there, the tears flowed freely. There was no plan B, only plan A, and that was Beijing. I was almost 47, and I didn't think I could keep training like I had been. Maybe it was time to give up this dream and get back to real life. So many thoughts were running through my head, but the one that stood out was that I felt I had let people down. My family, all those friends and coaches who had helped me so much, I felt like I had failed them. That night, there was a lot of beer consumed by the crew, trying to drown our disappointment.

A few days later, I wrote a blog about it, apologising for letting everyone down. I was done. I felt like I couldn't do it anymore. That is until my sister sent me an email telling me basically to pull my head out of the dirt! She told me that I hadn't disappointed anyone and that it wasn't about the final destination at all, but about the journey. She went on to explain that I had taken my readers on the most amazing journey and that if I loved rowing, then I should just row, continue that journey and not look at the destination. She said to take it a day at a time, a month at a time and a year at a time, that destinations could always change.

Life As A Rower

She was right. I did love rowing, and I would continue to row, making the team again the following year for the World Championships. These were in Poznan, Poland, and although we now had a different crew, we had done more training together. Three of us — myself, Pete Siri and Lisa Brown — were from the previous year, but to this team was added Alexandra (Alex) Green and Henry Macphillamy. We were excited to be there.

In the heats, only the first boat would get right through. We had placed second so had to go to the repêchage and won that race. We were so excited about heading to the final at the World Championships. The night before our race, we were called together by our coach, and what he said absolutely turned my stomach. He told us that we should be happy to have just made the final. We had exceeded his expectations and shouldn't expect any more than what we had done. Now, how the hell is that good coaching?

After our team meeting, I told the entire crew to meet in my room in ten minutes. When they arrived, I told them, 'I don't know about you guys, but I didn't come here just to be happy with being in the final. Anything can happen in a race, and I want us to do the best that we possibly can. How are the rest of you feeling?' There was consensus amongst us that we would do the best possible, but I believe that the coach had already put a seed of doubt in our mind.

Race day had arrived, and the weather had completely changed. Where we had rowed into headwinds the whole week, we now had a massive tailwind, which changed the dynamics altogether. We started off, and about 100 metres into the race, Pete, who was sitting in front of me, caught a crab, which caused his oar to be sucked under the water and was almost perpendicular to our boat. It was so violent that it threw him backwards and onto my lap. Henry, who was blind and partially deaf, didn't know what had happened and kept on rowing, which caused our boat to move into the lane beside us. Thank goodness, the other crew from that lane where ahead of us; otherwise there would have been an almighty crash. Lisa, our coxswain, was trying to get Henry's attention to stop rowing. When she finally did, we were able to slowly get Pete's oar out of the water. But by this time, the other crews were way down the course. As we started to row again, I didn't know if Alex, who was sitting behind me, was crying or laughing at the situation — it turned out she was in tears. Pete, in front of me, was swearing with each stroke of the oar; Henry just kept rowing, and Lisa was trying her best to keep us together and focused once again.

It was not how we wanted the final to work out, but as I said to everyone later that night: 'Hey, we placed sixth in the world!' And I was proud of that fact. With much less training as a crew together, we had two really great races and one bad one. It just so happened that the bad one was in the final. I was confident that, with the next three years to train together, we would be ready for the 2012 London Paralympic Games.

But, again, I was hit with a roadblock — and that was the sport itself and the people running it. The coach we had at the time certainly wasn't interested in our crew, as he had proved in Poznan, and put up so many barriers for us. We were losing crew members, who were going to other things in life, and it was at this time that Alex switched to cycling. She called me and told me that there was a category for trikes. I had purchased one and was using it as cross training and to ride to rowing training. This was in January of 2011, and she suggested that I come up to Queensland in April for the Australian Para-cycling National Championships. Cycling? I didn't know anything about racing my trike!

This proved to me that no matter how prepared you are for something, things can go wrong. It is important to believe in your abilities and not to let someone else's beliefs hold you back. Positively encouraging someone can be the best gift you can give them and can change their destiny.

CHAPTER 21

Cycling Journey

'It's a simple machine that conjures a vast mix of emotions. It can evoke the senses and raise the spirits. There's no better sensation than being on top of your gear making mountains feel like flat roads. Cycling throws up plenty of obstacles, unknown territory, high speed split-second considerations. Where to next? What's around the corner? Who cares, you're flyin'!'
~ CADEL EVANS

Over the course of the next couple of months, Alex convinced me that I should come to race at the nationals. The races were being held at the Glass House Mountains in Queensland. My 22-kilogram steel-framed trike had to get shipped up and back by truck, but I wasn't going to let that stop me. So began my introduction into cycling racing!

I met Alex up in Queensland, and with the van I had rented, we decided to have a look at the course. Both of us were stunned as we drove around. We looked at each other, thinking the same thing.

'How the hell am I going to get up those hills?' we both blurted out.

'I'll probably be walking and pushing my trike up here,' I said, laughing.

She agreed that she probably would too. I kept thinking what have I gotten myself into? We headed back to our accommodation and got ready to race the time trial the next day, which, thankfully, was flat.

After the time trial, the head coach, Peter Day, came over to me.

'Where did you come from?' he asked excitedly.

'Melbourne,' I replied.

'No, I mean as a cyclist,' said Peter.

'Oh, I'm not a cyclist. I'm a rower who is just having a bit of fun,' I said.

'No, you are a cyclist,' Peter replied. 'And the fastest T2 Woman I have ever seen. You have just smashed the qualifying speed for the national team for WT2.'

'Oh really, what is that?' I asked.

With a roll of his eyes, a shrug of his shoulders and an exasperated expression on his face, he told me it was just above an average speed of 24.5 km/h. I had averaged 27.85.

'I think I need to talk to your coach,' he said.

'Well, keep talking because I am my coach,' I said, pointing to my chest.

Peter just laughed, shook his head and said, 'We will have to talk later.'

That weekend, I raced two races, the time trial and the road race. There were only two of us in the trike category, me and Stephen. During the road race, we stayed pretty much together and towards the end of the race had one last big hill to climb, which was about 2 km long. It was one of the hills that Alex and I had commented on while doing a drive of the course. This is where Stephen took off as I struggled up the hill. Hills were not my forte. My trike was 22 kg; Steve's was 15 kg, and I had about another 20 kilos on me.

I could see him putting distance between us every 50 metres. As I got to the top of the hill, I only had about 1.5 km to go to the end of the race and I could see Stephen. I guess he figured that he had put enough distance between us on the climb and was taking it easy towards the finish. This is where my competitive mind came into play. There was a slight downhill to the finish, so I just kicked myself into another gear and went after him.

He hadn't looked back at all, and with about 30 metres to go to the finish, I was beside him. He was shocked and tried to kick it up a gear, but I had the momentum, crossing the line just millimetres in front of him, about half the width of a tire. The difference was one second. I wasn't sure how he was going to react as he had been riding and racing for a number of years, but he was gracious in defeat and was elated that he had someone to race. To me, this was thrilling — the fierceness of competition and never giving up. It felt like the tortoise and the hare story! It whetted my appetite for what might be possible and was the start of what would become an incredible sporting career. I decided that I needed to have an actual cycling coach, and it was then that Helen Kelly took over coaching duties.

Because of the speed that I had shown in the time trial, I was named on the national team for the upcoming World Cup, which, for the first time, was being held in Australia, in Sydney, in less than a month's time. This time, there would be no transporting my trike by truck. I was able to drive up to Sydney. But on the way, I got an itch on my back, that feeling of being bitten by something, and within a day, I had a rash across the right side of my back and side, just along the bra line. I happened to show it to one of the other cyclists who was a doctor, and she told me I had shingles. I was given the option of not competing, but as I said to Peter, 'I didn't drive over 1,000 km not to compete!'

I also got internationally classified at the event, which was great as it meant that I fit into the classification perfectly and was

A New Life Begins

allowed to race at an international level now. I was also rooming with one of the best female Para-cyclist that Australia had at the time, and as I was just about to race my fifth and sixth races ever, I was hoping for some guidance.

The night before the road race, she asked me how I was going to race the road race. I laughed and said I had no idea but that the men's world champion, David Stone, was racing as well, so I figured I would just try to follow him, stick to him like glue. I thought that would be a good tactic. We were lying in our beds in the dark, she laughed and said, 'Carol, he's a real athlete.' That comment stunned me; it was like being hit in the guts. I couldn't understand how a teammate could be so negative. Yes, I was new to cycling, and I was much heavier than I am now and certainly not as fit as I could have been, but that night, as I tried to sleep, all I could think was maybe she's right. What am I doing here? I had to do some serious self-talking to get that negative feeling out of me. Here I was, hoping for a mentor to help me along and advise me on how I might tackle the race, but all I got was a put-down.

The next day, as we lined up at the start of the race, I was put right next to David Stone. As soon as we headed off, I put my plan into action, to stay with him as long as I could. It was the only plan I had, but it didn't last too long! That didn't dissuade me from digging deep and giving it everything I had. I ended up working with a few of the other riders for the entire race and was the first woman to cross the line, winning my first ever international road race. I had given it my all, and I took back my self-belief, that belief my parents had instilled in me all those years ago. One person had almost taken that from me with one statement. I don't know if she even knew what she had said, or how devastating it could have been.

It was a successful couple of days, winning my first two World Cup gold medals. Before driving home, as I stood waiting to get a coffee in the hotel, Peter, who was standing beside me, leaned over.

'So, are you a cyclist or a rower?' he asked.

'Well, it looks like I'm a cyclist!' I said with a laugh.

And with that statement, I started training for the next couple of months for my first Para-cycling World Championships.

The World Championships were being held in Roskilde, Denmark, at the beginning of September 2011, so I didn't have much time to get ready. I was extremely confident going into the championships as Peter had told me that I was the fastest female T2 rider he had ever heard of. So I guess, in my pig-headedness and stubbornness, I just assumed that I would win! Boy, did I get a lesson.

A Canadian woman by the name of Marie-Eve Croteau had probably also been told she was the fastest. And she was! She beat me in the time trial by a whopping 31.32 seconds, and after that race, I was really down. I remember looking at the results as Peter came up to me, congratulating me for a great ride. I told him I was disappointed, and he reminded me that it was my first world championship and I had just won silver! I had beaten the reigning world champion, who had placed third, and a number of other women. I went back to the hotel and had to really do some self-talk. Silver was a really great starting point. It took me back to that first swimming race where I won a green ribbon and I had wanted red. I now wanted gold! I was new to this sport and now knew what I would have to do to get better, stronger and faster.

In the road race, she again killed me by a huge margin of 5 minutes and 52 seconds, but once again I won the silver medal. Not too bad to go home with two silver medals and now being second in the world!

Just before we were about to head back to Australia, Peter and Tom Skulander (the assistant head coach) sat me down for a debrief about the races. At the end, Peter said to me, 'If you go home, train hard, come back stronger and fitter, I will build you a new trike.' Well, this certainly was an incentive. My trike weighed

A New Life Begins

22 kg compared to the 15 kg all the others were racing on. I also weighed at least 20 kg more than my competitors. So getting fitter and stronger to lose the weight from myself and the trike was the goal.

By Christmas that year, I was down 15 kg in my body weight, and by March of 2012, Peter was true to his word and presented me with a new trike at a training camp we had in Canberra. I was over the moon and so excited to start training and racing on this new machine.

Like my mother and grandfather before me, life was about 'chasing my dreams'. I was 50 years old, and I felt like my world was just opening up with so many possibilities. I had great teachers who taught me that if I wanted something, I should go after it. Don't worry about failing, just use those failures as lessons, stepping stones towards your ultimate goal. And, like my sister taught me, 'Enjoy the journey, for those destinations can constantly change.'

My world was about to change as the world of Para-cycling opened up to me, and I could not even imagine how much!

CHAPTER 22
Chasing The Ultimate Dream

'Dreams are the seeds of change. Nothing ever grows without a seed, and nothing ever changes without a dream.'
~ DEBBY BOONE

From the beginning of my life with MS, I had said that I wanted to dictate what I could and couldn't do, not let MS do that for me. I had now represented Australia in rowing and cycling. But my ultimate goal was the 2012 London Paralympics. It had been a dream of mine for 41 years, across two countries and three sports. I was well on track and hopeful to make the team, although the Australian Para-cycling team was one of the hardest to make for the games. There were only six female spots, and with thirteen categories, you had to be at the top of your game.

On Friday 13 April, while on the Sunshine Coast in Queensland for the Australian National Championships, I received a letter advising me that I had been nominated for the 2012 Paralympic team.

A New Life Begins

I couldn't believe it. I had received the sixth and final spot on the team. My dream to represent my country at the highest level was about to come true.

My excitement was short-lived as I was advised a day later by Peter, our head coach, that one of the other cyclists was going to appeal my selection. She felt that she had the right to be on the team instead of me. The dream I had my entire life was just about to be realised, and it could now all coming crashing down. Unfortunately, the woman who had appealed was a rower whom Alex and I had beaten out of a seat in the boat for the 2009 World Championships. When she didn't get the seat, she had switched to cycling. Now she had missed her chance again, with Alex and I named on the team for London.

I had raced nationals that week and was 5 km an hour faster than the year before on the same course. I was happy about that, as were the coaches. But once I was home and received the appeals papers, reality hit me hard. I might not be going to London. The appeal was really an attack on me personally, talking about my age, my MS, and how I was untested against the men. In my category, there were not enough women to have our own races, so we would be racing against the men, with factoring put in place. It made me feel like this was revenge for beating her out of the rowing seat.

Two weeks after my notice of nomination, I was in an appeals tribunal to argue my case. The case took two hours to hear, and we were asked to leave for a half hour and then return for the finding of the panel. When we came back and I sat in my chair to hear my fate, to say I was nervous is an understatement. In my heart, I really wanted to hear that I was on the team; in my head, I knew the opposite was possible. My palms were sweaty and my heart was beating fast when the chair of the panel starting speaking. He advised that this couldn't be about personalities or personal attacks. The appeal had to be about the selection process and whether the selectors had followed the right process. He stated that he wasn't the person to decide who should be nominated, but he just had to look at the process. As far as he and the panel were concerned, the process had been followed. He then advised us that the appeal was to be dismissed. I was back on the team!

I headed to my car, got in and promptly burst into tears of relief. My dream was going to finally come true. Talk about a rollercoaster ride over the last two weeks. Now I was free to concentrate on training and the final touches, heading over to Europe to race in France and Spain at the World Cup.

I had some great racing in France, then won the time trial and was second behind Marie-Eve in the road race at the World Cup in Segovia, Spain. We were able to calculate the factoring for London against the men at the World Cup, which showed I had a little time to make up if I wanted to win in London.

We visited the Brands Hatch Circuit, where the road racing for the Paralympics was going to be held. There was an open day for Para-cyclists from around the world and we were able to ride the course. It was fabulous to be able to know what the course was going to be like for the games. We then headed home for one last month of training before heading back for the games.

I was so excited to be included in the team and wanted to make sure that I left nothing out of my training. On 5 August 2012, I took part in a time trial on the Kew Blvd near my home. During the race, on the return to the start, I lost control on the bend on a steep downhill and came off the trike, flying over the handlebars. Luckily, I turned my head but landed on my left hip, flipping on to my chest. With the trike still attached to my feet, I slid down the road. I thought I had broken my hip and felt like I couldn't breathe, but eventually I stopped sliding. My first thought was, 'Oh no, there goes London.' My second was to try and get off the road before a car came around the bend, as the road was still open to cars.

A New Life Begins

I got myself moved off the road, took stock of what my injuries were and just wanted to try and get back on the trike to finish. To this day I can't remember who it was, but someone helped me get the chain back on, get on the trike and slowly ride to the finish line. It was hard riding, getting my hip to move, and I could only use one arm on the bars as my chest was so sore. But I did make it back to the finish, then fell in a heap. People I knew helped get my trike on the back of my car, helped me with ice on my injuries, and then I headed home, feeling like I had been hit by a bus. I hadn't lost any skin, and because I was able to slowly ride and walk, I realised my hip wasn't broken, just bruised.

As it turned out, I had cracked my third rib, bruised my chest terribly and bruised my left hip worse. My best friend became an ice pack. I also let Peter Day, our head coach, know what had happened, but my body healed over the next few weeks before the games. The one thing that I had to get right was my head.

After the crash, I was a bit wary of getting back on the trike. Even though I had finished the race, I was scared and worried about riding down the huge hills in the course at the games. It was a real mental fight to get myself back to where I was before the crash. I have our mechanic, Dan Brent, to thank for being my riding partner those few weeks in France at our training camp before the games. He really helped me to overcome my fears and anxieties about going downhill fast.

The day of the time trial at the 2012 London Paralympic Games came around very fast. In the time trial, all riders go off at one-minute intervals, and at 4.55 pm I was the last Australian to race on the day. I was the sixth last rider to start. David Stone, the past world champion, was starting one minute behind me, so I wanted to use that as motivation. I had done my homework; I knew how fast David and Hans-Peter Durst, the world champion, could go. I was aware that I had to stay in front for as long as possible. I also had Marie-Eve, of Canada, who had beaten me the year before, starting second last.

I worked out where I believed David would pass me on the course so aimed to make it past that point before he caught me.

At the start of the race, I passed three riders within a very short time and kept thinking about how much I believed in my ability and myself. I also repeated stay in front of David, stay in front of David in my head. He didn't catch me at the point I expected him to, which was fantastic and spurred me on. But then, out of nowhere, he caught me, not that far from the finish. I had two hills to conquer and could not let him get too far away from me.

The noise down the finishing straight was incredible, with people cheering and pounding on the side boards. You could actually feel the noise pounding through your body. I could see the finish line and powered towards it. Then all of a sudden, it was over. I knew I had given it my all as I had nothing left in the tank. I couldn't even pedal to our bay in the sheds. My legs were spent, and I was lucky our physiotherapist was there to push me along.

Now it was a waiting game. I had no idea what time David had done, and there were still other riders to come — including good riders from Italy, Canada, France and Germany — who could pip me at the post. I found out, after I had finished, that Marie-Eve had not started due to a head injury she had acquired from a crash during a training ride.

In our shed, trying to cool down, I couldn't hear the results being announced, but our media manager, Genny Sheer, was looking at them on her phone.

'I think you've got this,' she said, but I put my hand up to her.

'I don't want to hear,' I said. 'I need to have everyone finished and hear it over the speaker.'

I kept riding for a few more minutes until the head coach of the British team came in and put his hand out to me.

'Congratulations!' he said.

'What for?' I asked.

A New Life Begins

'You've just won!'

I shook his hand, bewildered, and promptly burst into tears, looking at Genny.

'I've been trying to tell you for the last five minutes that you had won!' she said, smiling.

Peter Day, who was still our head coach, came in and gave me the biggest bear hug you can imagine, while I sat on the trainer with my legs spinning around.

David Stone had ended up in third place, with Hans-Peter Durst, from Germany, in second. Both men were extremely courteous and supportive in congratulating me on the win. Not only had I finally had my life-long dream come true, but I had capped it off with a gold medal as well. I always say that the medal was the icing on the cake. If I hadn't won, I would still have been successful. What mattered was that I had done my best and had finally represented my country at the highest pinnacle of sport.

The best part about the win was that my mother, Aunt Marjorie and my sister, Cindy, were there to see it happen. Mom, who had been up all those early mornings to drive me to swim training and had pushed me to pursue another sport, well, it was her win as well. Approaching my family to hugs and tears of joy after the medal ceremony was overwhelming. I was sad that my dad wasn't there because of his health, but I was able to call him later to tell him. Russ, at home in Australia, was so excited when I called him. He told me he loved me, said to rest up and enjoy the accolades, and wished me the best of luck for the road race. The next day, I was allowed to leave the village to meet up with my family for a celebratory lunch. It was wonderful to spend some quality time with them, in amongst all the media interviews I then was doing.

The road race was two days later. This time it was not factored, so I had to race the men on equal terms. I was pretty happy with how I performed. I was able to keep up fairly well with the men, but towards the end, the fastest riders dropped me and a number of others. We worked well towards the finish, and in the end, I was seventh across the line and the first woman. I couldn't have asked for a better campaign.

The question was: where to now? I had reached my dream, so it was time to set another goal. I still had not been crowned world champion, so that would be the new challenge. I decided to follow the advice from my sister all those years before about taking the journey and enjoying each day as it came.

The next few years were beyond what I ever expected. I won a number of world championships in both the time trial and the road race, with one little hiccup in 2015, when I was beaten in the road race by a new rider from the USA.

It had taken a long time, but I learned that dreams can come true if you believe in yourself and your abilities. Never give up!

CHAPTER 23

The Road To Rio

'She believed she could, so she did.'
~ R.S. GREY

The Paralympic Games bring out a whole different level of competition. For athletes, it is the culmination of years of training focused on just that one goal and on the ultimate prize, the gold medal. Schooling, careers and lives are put on hold to concentrate on one objective: stepping on that podium. As an elite athlete, you become selfish, but not in a bad way. It is all about getting the best out of yourself. So, other matters in life are pushed to the side, and especially in the last year of the four-year cycle, everything is timed right down to that one race.

As we were getting closer to the 2016 Rio Paralympics, I couldn't believe that I would be seeing my dream come true for a second time. I had followed my sister's advice and just enjoyed the journey, and here we were again. These games were going to be a bit more emotional as I had lost my dad in March of that year and he wasn't going to be around to see what I could accomplish. He and Mom had always been so supportive of anything that I tried to do.

These games were also going to be different in that women were having their own races. I felt like I had to change the way I raced so that the other girls wouldn't know what to expect. I had come second the year before in the road race, and to be honest, I was more focused on the time trial. Having won it in 2012 and having to race the men, I really wanted to put my stamp on it. If I could win the road race as well, it would be incredible.

I worked with my coach, Rebecca DiCello, and my sport scientist, Nick Owen, from the Victorian Institute of Sport on how to race completely differently, not leading from the front, as usual, but tactfully being able to know when to take off and drop all the other girls. As Rio got closer, I became more competent at my sprinting ability and knowing when to make the jump, so I was feeling more confident.

We had all worked hard. There was that special feeling you get in a hard training session when you think you have nothing left, but you find that little bit extra to push yourself up that steep hill or make that last sprint faster. There was also the excitement you feel on the start ramp, when you take those last few deep breaths, calming yourself, knowing that you are ready. The hard training has been done, and you are focused on what you have to do. This is how I felt in Rio.

The day of the time trial arrived, and I was the last rider to head off. The course was set with the beach on one side, which, on most days, is a beautiful sight, and with favelas on the other, which was such a contrast of living conditions. Luckily, I had been able to have a look at the area before race day, so it was all about focusing on what I had to do.

We knew it would most likely be windy, but I don't think I expected it to be as windy as it was. As I hit the turn-around point to head back to the finish line, the wind caught me, pushing me off to the right and making me feel like I was going to get blown off the road. I couldn't stay in the aerobars and had to revert to the bullhorns to pull the trike back to the centre of the road, then get back in the aerobars.

As I crossed the finish line, I was so focused that I had no idea what was around me, who I passed, who I didn't, and when I finished. I really had no idea where I had placed.

I was met by our physiotherapist, Eliza, after the finish line and wrapped in a cold wet towel, got my helmet off and waited to hear the results. I saw one of my competitors, Jill, from the USA, just down from me, and one of her support staff started whooping, hollering and celebrating. Then just up from her, the team around my Canadian competitor, Shelley Gautier, was hugging and congratulating her. At this point, I looked at Eliza with a questionable look as if to say … where the hell did I come?

She shrugged her shoulders and said, 'I have no idea where you placed.'

There were celebrations happening all around me, and I started panicking that I hadn't placed at all. Eliza's phone rang, and I could hear her talking to someone, at which point I heard her say, 'Do you know where Carol placed?'

There was silence, then, 'Oh, okay.'

It didn't sound good at all. I could feel the tears welling up in my eyes, and my heart felt like it was beating out of my chest. I waited to hear the bad news.

Eliza hung up and put her phone in her pocket. She looked at me.

'Well, where did I place?' I asked.

She smiled and said, 'You won!'

Oh my god, the relief was enormous as I burst into tears and Eliza hugged me. It had been Peter on the phone, wondering where we were, she told me. As we headed off the road towards the barriers, one of the media personnel from Paralympics Australia, who was standing there with a camera, asked why we hadn't been celebrating. I turned to him and said that I didn't think I had won a medal — let alone, the event.

We got back to our tent to find everyone there celebrating. When Eliza explained that we didn't know where I had placed, Peter gave me another one of his bear hugs.

'Silly woman,' he said, 'didn't you see how many people you passed?'

Pete had been in my follow car during the race, but, no, I really hadn't seen anything. I had been so 'in the zone' and concentrating on what I was doing that I had no idea. As it turned out, I had beaten Jill by 38 seconds, so it truly was a great win.

I now had a day to reset before the road race. I was more relaxed going into this race as my goal of winning the time trial had been reached, but I was a bit nervous of racing in a new way.

The next day, as we lined up for the road race, I could feel the butterflies in my stomach. I knew I was ready, but this new way of racing was untested. All the women would have been expecting me to go off the front, but when the gun went, I didn't move. Instead, I let them all take off and then slid in at the back. Suffice to say that there was a bit of yelling from some of the front riders telling me to take a turn at the front. I had taken my turn when the German competitor, Jana, took off, and no one chased her, so off I went to chase her down, with a trail of riders sitting in behind me. But I didn't want to be on the front of the pack, so with a bit of ingenuity, I pretended to slam on my brakes, which sent riders scurrying around me, and I slid in behind them. This was one of the scenarios that Nick and I had worked on.

At about 6.5 km to go, I was sitting right behind Jill, and over the next minute or so, I saw her take a drink of water, pull her jersey down at the back and then watch her change gears and I thought she's getting ready to take off. It was a bit farther out than I wanted to go, but with 5.5 km to go, I waited for the girls to weave to the right and sprinted to the very far-left side of the road. I wanted to get away before Jill, and it was my plan to sprint as hard as I could for 40 seconds without looking back. I thought my lungs and head were going to explode!

After about 45 seconds, I looked back to see if anyone had come with me. Jill had tried to, but I could see that if I kept it up, I was going to break that invisible bungee cord that was between us. There was a right-hand turn up around a 'dog leg' section, where I kept the pressure up, not looking back once. As I came back down this section, I could see that she was about 300 metres behind, and none of the other girls were with her. I then had only about 600 metres to go to the finish. On the second last corner, Peter Day was standing there, screaming at me to take the last corner carefully. I was way ahead, but I wasn't there to take anything slowly. Those last few hundred metres, I gave it all I had, getting around the last corner safely. I sprinted to the finish line with a feeling of satisfaction and overwhelming relief that my tactics had worked.

I had finished in Rio with two gold medals and my dream having come true for the second time. I couldn't have asked for any more.

My family before me had instilled in me that I could chase any dream I wanted and that nothing was impossible. They had all chased their own dreams and accomplished them. Cindy had taught me that if I enjoyed the journey, I did not need to worry about the destination because it would come, and boy, did it ever. They have taught me that having self-belief was something I carried with me. I just didn't expect it to take me so long to achieve it!

CHAPTER 24

Adversity Into Advantage

'Don't let the force of an impression when it first hits you knock you off your feet; just say to it: Hold on a moment; let me see who you are and what you represent. Let me put you to the test.'
~ EPICTETUS

After my initial diagnosis of multiple sclerosis and taking about six months to really come to terms with it, I always knew that I wanted to take this adverse change in my life and use it to my advantage. I had learned from my brother, Brian, that having a 'disability' didn't mean the end of the world and that I could accomplish anything I set my mind to, as he had done.

I had proven this by representing my country, fulfilling that lifelong dream. Sure, it wasn't for Canada, it was for Australia. It wasn't the Olympics, it was the Paralympics. It wasn't in swimming, it was in cycling – and it wasn't wearing red and white, but green and gold. But I had done it and been lucky enough to do it twice!

A New Life Begins

I had also been able to find purpose in life when I accidentally started a charity event called the 24 Hour Mega Swim. The MS Society of Victoria, as it was known when I was diagnosed, had been so helpful to me, and I had become involved with a number of aspects within the MS community. There was one tireless worker, Jo Fairbairn, who had been told to raise money one year but hadn't been told what to do with it afterwards. She had raised $10,000 through a luncheon she had held so came up with a program called The Go For Gold Scholarships. These were $2,000 scholarships that people living with MS could apply for to follow a dream. There were five on offer the first year, and the second year, she found funding to have another five awarded. However, in the third year, she couldn't find a backer and approached me to help her figure out how we might raise the money.

I was working for Australia Post at the time and knew that there was a chance to apply for funding through the company's philanthropic arm, so we put together a proposal and presented it to the board. We, unfortunately, lost out to an Adopt a Dolphin project, which to this day boggles my mind. I knew of a number of people working for Australia Post who had MS and thought it would be a no-brainer to contribute to a charity that supported some of their employees. But it was not to be and made me look for other alternatives.

One of the scholarships to be awarded was in the category of sport. So I approached my Masters swim club president and suggested that our club organise a 24-hour swimming relay to try and raise at least $2,000 for that category. She promptly agreed and suggested that we invite other clubs and try to raise the whole $10,000. I did tell her that it would be a huge undertaking, but she assured me that she and the club would be there to help along the way.

I was able to secure the Fitzroy swimming pool for free from the City of Yarra and had sent out invites to many other clubs and organisations to take part. However, the club president promptly quit, and I was left on my own! I was able to rope in five friends, who assisted me and helped me put together a successful event. The ten teams that took part surpassed my expectations. We had raised $22,000, which I happily handed over to Jo, excited that she now had two years' worth of funding to run the program. My job had been done, and as I handed out some awards at the end of the swim, someone yelled from the back, 'When is it next year?'

Next year … you have got to be kidding, I thought! This was a tough gig to put together, and as I told everyone that it was a one-off event, the protests were loud. Many participants told me I had to do it again; they had really enjoyed it.

I took a few days to think about it, chatted with the friends who had helped me and decided that if we could raise $22,000 in one day in the first year, we could do even better the second year. I even turned to the Rotary Club of Fitzroy to see if they would assist me with providing food for the participants. One of the women in the club, Anne Davie, stood up right away and said, 'I'll do the roster.' This was the start of an amazing friendship with Anne, who took the reins for the next 19 years feeding all the participants for 24 hours and feeding them for free.

The second year turned into a third year and continued until we had our 20th annual swim at the Fitzroy pool, in February 2020. The event grew throughout the eastern seaboard, with other swims throughout Victoria, New South Wales, Tasmania and the Australian Capital Territory. We even had a few in South Australia and Queensland for a couple of years until those MS societies decided to try it on their own.

The scholarships had even benefited me. In 2005, I applied for one to go to the World Masters Games, which were being held in Edmonton, Canada. For the first time ever, the Masters Games had Para sports. It was through these games, as a Para-swimmer, that I gained the recognition of Paralympics Australia and was invited to the talent search day that set me on my path to becoming a Paralympian. So, the scholarships really did turn lives around.

I had found my passion. I had seen what the scholarships could accomplish and was fully committed to handing out as many of them as possible to help make living with MS that little bit better. To date, the swims have raised just over $11 million, helping fund over 1,000 scholarships, a financial assistance program and a number of self-help courses all run by MS.

By 2020, I decided that my time to retire from running the Fitzroy event had come, so we made it a huge party, with the teams raising just under $125,000. It was a great way to leave the event in the hands of what is now called MS Limited (MSL). I had been able to entrench the Go For Gold Scholarships into the business of MSL and felt that I had made my contribution to life with MS.

In return for my work, fundraising for MS and my gold medal in London, I was made a Member of the Order of Australia in 2014, which was an amazing honour from my adopted country that I now called home. Without having been diagnosed with multiple sclerosis, none of this would have happened.

Without turning that adversity into an advantage, I would never have become a Paralympian. I wouldn't have become an author, and the money that has been raised through my charity event wouldn't have happened. I wouldn't have met the people who have become lifelong friends, not only in Australia, through rowing and cycling, but across the world. I never would have become a speaker for a wide range of audiences, from children right through to huge corporations. I wouldn't be a director on the board of Cycling Victoria or a member of the Paralympics Australia Athletes Commission. Without the adversity I have been through, I don't think I would be the person I have become.

Life can certainly throw us curveballs at times, but I believe that we can thrive in the uncomfortable moments that those adversities bring us. Although it may be difficult to believe at the time, I am living proof that you can use any adversity to your advantage — but only if you chose to look at it that way. As Warren Macdonald, a good friend of mine, taught me: 'It's not what you see; it's how you see it.'

Adversity can make or break us, so next time you are faced with a challenge, what will you do? Will you accept it, use your adversity to your advantage and forge on to amazing success? Or will you back away and let opportunity pass you by?

Overcoming adversity wasn't something I was born with; I learned it through my grandfather overcoming the loss of a leg to lead an incredible life. I learned it through my brother, who overcame doctors and went on to live a life of passion and full of love despite being told, from the moment he was born, that he would never live a normal life. And I learned it through my mother, who taught me to 'think outside the box' when challenges where put in front of me.

> 'You should never view your challenges as a disadvantage. Instead, it's important for you to understand that your experience facing and overcoming adversity is actually one of your biggest advantages.'
> ~ MICHELLE OBAMA

CONCLUSION

Today, 25 August 2020, should have marked the opening of the Tokyo Paralympics. For me, the year 2020 was probably going to be my last Paralympic Games. I would be 59, and I didn't think I had another one in my sights. So, I told myself this was going to be my best year ever.

My goal was to come away with another gold medal, to add to the three I already had. I had been unbeaten in the time trial over the last two games — London and Rio — so I wanted another one in Tokyo. Even though I had won the road race in Rio, it was going to be hard to do it again. Pulling off a gold medal would certainly have been a bonus. But the Time Trial was my target. My dreams for this year have been shattered by the pandemic that is sweeping the world.

I certainly know that there is something bigger than the Paralympics happening; it is called 'Life'. I know that there are people out there who are having the worst day of their life or even the last day of their life. So I am one of the lucky ones. I haven't been touched by the pandemic personally: my family is safe, I have a roof over my head and a fridge full of food. But it still hurts to have the last four years of training be put on hold or maybe lost forever.

Although in my heart I am hoping that the games go ahead next year, in my head, it doesn't seem possible. This will probably be my last games, and to think that they might not happen at all, even a year late, is very sad. It is not the way I wanted to finish my career.

I realise that I am only able to get through this because of the lessons I have learned from my family and from my own experiences — lessons about perseverance, resilience, determination and courage, about empathy, integrity, compassion and commitment.

I count myself lucky because my parents always impressed upon me that I could do anything or be anything in life that I wanted to. I was never told that I couldn't do something because I was a girl. My mother proved that she could be a trailblazer as the fourteenth woman to join the Toronto Police, so why couldn't her daughters do whatever they wanted?

During the course of my life, I have been able to have a number of careers and have enjoyed each and every one of them because they were my choice. My family might not have agreed with all my choices, as I might not have agreed with all theirs, but they always respected me for the choices I made, and vice versa.

My family also instilled in me a sense of adventure and the courage to leave the shore, to take a chance in a new world. Every single one of them has lived their lives like mini-adventures: grandparents who sailed across the world to start a new life, parents who tried so many different jobs, a sister who reinvented herself after years in one career to find something that she loved and was happy doing — and Brian, who never let his disability define who he was.

My own experiences with travelling and with my careers have also provided me with unexpected insight and wisdom. My life has certainly been interesting. It's had adventure, adversity, love, success, failure and excitement. All of this has enabled me to become the person that I am today.

Without these life lessons, I would never have got through my diagnosis of multiple sclerosis like I did, nor the ovarian cancer scare, and I certainly wouldn't be a Paralympian and world champion in cycling. Thanks to these lessons, I was able to choose how I wanted to live through these adversities. So I thank them for that.

I was taught to always do your best, no matter what that is. If you can look back on a test in school, a career choice or a race and know that you have given it your all, then that is all that matters. I think I have always taken it one step further, in that I have grown

Conclusion

to expect myself to exceed my expectations. Instead of aiming to give one hundred per cent, I try to give one hundred and fifty per cent. At least then I have left no stone unturned, and I can never have regret for anything I try to do.

I was lucky to have known my grandparents, all except Edna, but I believe that she left a bit of herself in my dad, which he passed down to me. I've inherited some great genes, which has provided me with an incredible life. Writing this book, I have learned more about my family than I had ever known. It has been extraordinary and has made me realise how lucky I am to have been born into such an amazing family — one that has now spanned three countries but has dedicated a total 85 years to serving one city, with pride.

ACKNOWLEDGEMENTS

First I must acknowledge my family for everything that they have brought to my life and the lessons they have taught me. For without those lessons I don't know how I would have coped with the adversity and change that has come into my life.

All the police officers I had the privilege to work with and for, taught me do the best job that I could possibly do. They instilled in me that drive to make sure that everything I did had a purpose, that I could possibly affect, for the good, the lives of others.

I also want to thank all those friends and coaches who have supported me across three sports and two countries. My earliest swimming coaches who instilled me that original work ethic which I was able to bring into my life later in my rowing and cycling lives. My first rowing coach Sally Shaw who saw something in me and believed that I could accomplish what I set out to do.

I would have never switched to cycling if my teammate and good friend Alexandra Lisney hadn't talked me into it and dragged me to my first nationals. And I don't know if I would have gone as far as I have in cycling if it wasn't for Peter Day proving to me that I could be one of the best and that I needed to get myself a cycling coach.

To my coaches Helen Kelly and Rebecca DiCello and sport scientist Nick Owen, I honestly would not have achieved what I have without your guidance and support. Thank you to AusCycling Victoria, AusCycling (formerly Cycling Australia) and all the staff, Tom, Muz, Mikey, Wazza, Cam, Nick, Dave, Keren and Berthy, who have been involved in my cycling career, for the support you have shown me over the last 10 years. Here's hoping there is at least a couple more years of competing!

I have been a part of so many teams through my swimming, rowing and cycling careers and all those teammates have, all each in their own way, taught me lessons over the years so a HUGE thank you to all of them.

This book wouldn't have been possible without the help of a number of family members who were able to supply me with stories from the past. Thanks to my aunts, Rheta Fines, Marjorie Jenkins, Betty Simmonds, my mother Phyllis and my sister Cynthia, for adding your memories to this book.

Thanks to my niece Jamie Farshchi, a writer herself, who assisted me with each chapter, editing as I wrote and telling me if I needed more or less in areas. You were a godsend during the process.

Thank you to my mentor for this book Andrew Jobling who made me believe that I had a story to get out to the public and that I could get it published.

I am grateful for the support I received from Luke Harris, who designed the front cover and to Mark Zocchi and all those at Brolga Publishing for believing in my book enough to want to publish it.

Finally, thank you to my husband Russell. We have had our ups and downs in the 26 years of marriage but we have always managed to come out the other side. Your support and belief in no matter what I want to attempt to do has been unwavering. I love you and promise that I won't keep racing and travelling the world for another 10 years. We have been able to make it through the last year almost 24/7 together thanks to COVID-19, so I think that when I finally do retire, we will be fine with each other's company!

CAROL'S ACCOMPLISHMENTS

Paralympic Games

Games	Event	Result
London 2012	Mixed T1-T2 Time Trial	Gold
London 2012	Mixed T1-T2 Road Race	7th(1st woman)
Rio de Janeiro 2016	Women's T1-T2 Time Trial	Gold
Rio de Janeiro 2016	Women's T1-T2 Road Race	Gold

World Championships

Year	Venue	Results
2011	Roskilde, Denmark	Silver – WT2 Time Trial
		Silver – WT2 Road Race
2012	Not held	
2013	Baie Comeau, Canada	Gold – WT2 Time Trial
		Gold – WT2 Road Race
2014	Greenville, USA	Gold – WT2 Time Trial
		Gold – WT2 Road Race
2015	Switzerland	Gold – WT2 Time Trial
		Silver – WT2 Road Race
2016	Not held	
2017	Pietermaritzburg, South Africa	Gold – WT2 Time Trial
		Gold – WT2 Road Race
2018	Maniago, Italy	Silver – WT2 Time Trial
		Silver – WTs Road Race
2019	Emmen, Netherlands	Gold – WT2 Time Trial
		Gold – Wt2 Road Race
2020	Not held	

World Cups

Date	Venue	Results
2011	Sydney, Australia	Gold both TT and Road Race
2012	Segovia, Spain	Gold – TT and Silver – Road Race
2013	Matane, Canada	Gold both TT and Road Race
2014	Segovia, Spain	Gold both TT and Road Race
2015	Elzach, Germany	Gold both TT and Road Race
	Pietermaritzburg, Sth Africa	Gold both TT and Road Race
2016	Oostende, Belgium	Gold both TT and Road Race
2017	Oostende, Belgium	Gold – TT and Silver – Road Race
	Maniago, Italy	Silver – TT and Bronze – Road Race
	Emmen, Netherlands	Gold both TT and Road Race
2018	Emmen, Netherlands	Gold – TT and Silver – Road Race
	Oostende, Belgium	Gold both TT and Road Race
	Baie Comeau, Canada	Gold – TT and Bronze – Road Race (overall World Cup Winner)
2019	Corridonia, Italy	Silver both TT and Road Race
	Oostende, Belgium	Gold both TT and Road Race
	Baie Comeau, Canada	Gold both TT and Road Race (overall World Cup Winner)

Other International Races

Year	Venue	Results
2016	Upper Austria Tour	GC Winner
2016	Cologne Classic, Germany	GC Winner
2017	Cologne Classic, Germany	GC Winner
2019	Upper Austria Tour	GC Winner
2019	Cologne Classic, Germany	GC Winner
2019	Swiss Serie, Switzerland	TT – 1st, Road Race – 1st

Carol's Accomplishments

Australian Championships

Year	Titles
2011	Time Trial and Road Race
2012	Time Trial and Road Race
2013	Time Trial and Road Race
2014	Time Trial and Road Race
2015	Time Trial and Road Race
2016	Time Trial and Road Race
2017	Time Trial and Road Race
2018	Time Trial and Road Race
2019	Time Trial and Road Race
2020	Time Trial and Road Race

Other Awards

Year	Award
2013/15/16/17/19	Australian Female Para Cyclist of the Year
2018	Victorian Female Para Cyclist of the Year
2017	Award of Excellence - Victorian Institute of Sport
2017	Masters Sportsperson of the Year Vic Disability Sport and Recreation
2016	Female Sportspersons of the Year & Masters Sportsperson of the Year Vic Disability Sport and Recreation
2015	Victorian Finalist - Australian of the Year
2014	Order of Australia - A Member of the Order of Australia (AM)
2013/16	Victorian Cyclist of the Year
2013	Top Elite Athlete with a Disability Victorian Institute of Sport
2011-17	Included in the Who's Who of Australian Women
2011	Minister for Health Volunteer Awards – Commendation
2010	Included in the Who's Who of Australian Women "hope & courage"

Other Awards (continued)

Year	Award
2009	John Studdy Award from MS Australia
2008	Included in the Inaugural Who's Who in Victoria and the Who's Who of Australian Women 2006 Victorian Masters Sportsperson of the Year
2006	Herald Sun Pride of Australia Awards Role Model Category
2003	The Rotary Foundation of Rotary International Named a Paul Harris Fellow
2001	Rotary International Shine on Award Certificate of Commendation

ORDER

THE FORCE WITHIN

Carol Cooke AM

ISBN: 9781920785031		Qty
RRP	AU$34.99	.....
Postage within Australia	AU$5.00	.....
	TOTAL* $_____	

*All prices include GST

Name: ....

Address: ....

....

Phone: ....

Email: ....

Payment: [ ] Money Order   [ ] Cheque   [ ] MasterCard   [ ] Visa

Cardholder's Name:..

Credit Card Number: ....

Signature:...

Expiry Date: ....

Allow 7 days for delivery.

Payment to: Marzocco Consultancy (ABN 14 067 257 390)
PO Box 452
Torquay Victoria 3228
Australia

BE PUBLISHED

Publish through a successful publisher.
Brolga Publishing is represented through:
• National book trade distribution, including sales, marketing & distribution through Simon & Schuster.
• International book trade distribution to:
    - The United Kingdom
    - Sales representation in South East Asia
• Worldwide e-Book distribution

For details and enquiries, contact:
Brolga Publishing Pty Ltd
ABN 46 063 962 443
PO Box 452
Torquay Victoria 3228
Australia

markzocchi@brolgapublishing.com.au
(Email for a catalogue request)

www.ingramcontent.com/pod-product-compliance
Lightning Source LLC
Chambersburg PA
CBHW020354170426
43200CB00005B/167